The Magic of Relaxation

TAI CHI & VISUALISATION EXERCISES FOR YOUNG CHILDREN

PATRICE THOMAS

Pademelon Press

First published in May, 2002 by
Pademelon Press
7/3 Packard Avenue
Castle Hill, New South Wales, 2154

© Patrice Thomas

Editing by Forsyth Editorial Services
Cover and page design by Tania Edwards
Printed in Australia by Ligare Pty Limited

Thomas, Patrice.
    The magic of relaxation : Tai Chi and visualisation exercises for young children.
    Bibliography.
    Includes index.
    ISBN 1 876138 12 2.
    1. Relaxation. 2. Stress management for children. 3. Tai chi chüan.
    I. Title.

613.7148

Foreword

Patrice Thomas has been a pioneer in the promotion of the importance of relaxation as a key life competence for young children. Building on the burgeoning literature on the long-term benefits of relaxation in countering the negative effects of stress, the author provides an important volume that will enable educators and parents to provide children with the skills to use relaxation as a means of enhancing their physical development, health and wellbeing. Patrice describes in clear detail the basic elements of Tai Chi and progressive relaxation and provides a very timely and practical resource. It should prove to be a valuable tool for those seeking to address children's emotional needs and their skills for coping. Relaxation training is a key element in the development of resilient, competent children who will be well-equipped to face and overcome the challenges of an increasingly stressful world. I congratulate Patrice Thomas and her publisher on an excellent addition to the literature.

Professor Alan Hayes
Dean and Head of Division
Australian Centre for Educational Studies
Macquarie University

Comments about the book

In my office at work I have a photograph of one of the children who do Tai Chi Ch'uan with Patrice Thomas. I have been refreshed by the image of this little Anglo-Australian boy doing Chinese relaxation exercise. Patrice would be modest of her accomplishments, but I for one am moved by this initiative of hers, uniquely Australian in that it represents an openness on the part of some people in this part of the world to learn from the wisdom of Asia. Our whole world is in dire need of positive, 'heart and soul' learning, and of teachers like Patrice Thomas. As someone who has been involved in promoting health-enhancing environments for 30 years, I encourage everyone who works with children to read this accessible, useful and inspiring book.

Professor John Macdonald
Foundation Chair — Primary Health Care
College of Social and Health Sciences
University of Western Sydney — Hawkesbury

This book is both fun to read and very practical in its suggestions. It offers a splendid resource for new ideas on encouraging young children's imagination and creativity. It also inspires reflection on ways of nurturing relaxation and wellbeing.

Dr Frank Hutchinson
Educationalist and Social Researcher
UWS — Hawkesbury

Offering a wealth of wisdom, this delightful book draws on Patrice's many years of experience in teaching Tai Chi and her dedication to sharing its magic with others. The very practical focus will be especially welcomed by parents and educators who are reaching out for ways to nurture young children's minds, bodies and souls.

Dr Jennifer Sumsion
Senior Lecturer
Institute of Early Childhood
Macquarie University

It is timely that a book such as this is now available to parents and teachers of young children. These days, children are swept along in the flurry of their parents' hurried lifestyles and in the routines of a busy, long day care or preschool setting. In most instances, it is rare that children have a moment for reflection or for simply 'just being'. With this book, the parent or teacher is ready to embark on many serene experiences with the young children in their care.

With their rhythm and gentle pace, Patrice's guiding words and meaningful phrases convey a calming effect to the reader. The visualisation exercises pave the way for the newcomer to try these techniques for helping children learn to relax and gain confidence as they progress through the book.

Relaxation is a life skill for all of us, it is wonderful that children will have the opportunity to develop skills which will assist in ensuring their health and wellbeing.

Wendy Shepherd
Director
Mia Mia Child and Family Studies Centre
Macquarie University

iv

Table of Contents

Foreword   iii
Comments about the book   iii
Acknowledgments   vii
Disclaimer   viii
Introduction   viii

Chapter 1: Transforming Stress in Young Children   1

How much daily relaxation time do your children have?
   A checklist for parents   2
Gentle exercise for body, mind and spirit   6
How relaxation helps children   8
Ask yourself: How can I develop an ecology of relaxation in my life?   8
   Personal … develop a 'relaxed way of being'   8
   Transforming stress into vitality   9
   Work environment   11
   An over-riding philosophy   13

Chapter 2: Getting Started   15

How to begin   16
   Provide a quite place   16
   Set the scene   16
   Music   17
   Entering the relaxation space   17
   Routine and ritual   17
The educator's/parent's role   18
   Important teacher qualities   19
Structure of the relaxation session   20
   Beginning circle   20
   Tai Chi exercises   20
   Progressive relaxation and visualisation   21
   Sharing circle   21
Managing children's behaviour   22
Helping parents to introduce relaxation techniques at home   25
   Beginning 'relaxation time' at home   26

Chapter 3: Gentle Tai Chi Exercises   27

Warm up exercises   28
   Cleansing breath   28
   Stretching the arms   29
   Waist swings   30
Tai Chi movements   31
   Movement 1: Wu Chi   32
   Movement 2: Expanding the heart   33
   Movement 3: Holding up heaven   34
   Movement 4: Turning the waist and pushing the palm   36

Movement 5: Painting a rainbow   37
Movement 6: Punching in a Horse Riding Stance   38
Movement 7: The bird   40
Movement 8: Stepping and bouncing a ball   41
Movement 9: Spinning silken threads from the bottom of the ocean   42
Movement 10: Salute to the sun   43

Chapter 4: Relaxation and Visualisation   **45**

What is progressive relaxation?   46
What is visualisation?   46
Ideas for spoken directions for a progressive relaxation exercise   47
Visualisation script 1: A walk in the rainforest   49
Visualisation script 2: My magical rainforest friend   52
Visualisation script 3: A flight with a magical bird   54
Visualisation script 4: A walk by the sea   56
Visualisation script 5: A walk to a mountain   57
Visualisation script 6: My symbol of peace   58
Visualisation script 7: Floating on a cloud   59
Visualisation script 8: White light of love   60
Visualisation script 9: My secret garden   61
Visualisation script 10: My boat on the lake   63

Chapter 5: Creative Expression   **65**

Building on relaxation exercises through the creative
    and expressive arts   67
General ideas for babies, toddlers and older children   75
For babies   75
For toddlers   75
Life learning   76
Creative expression   76
3 to 5 year-olds through to primary school   76

In conclusion   78
Appendix: Some answers to questions and concerns from
    educators and parents on using *The Magic of Relaxation*   79
Useful references   83
Useful music selections   85

Index   **87**

Acknowledgments

This book has been many years in the making. In my early years of teaching, I was initially inspired by the children and staff of a Special School. Noeleen O'Beirne, my dear friend and then Principal of the school, had the vision and courage to incorporate relaxation classes into the school curriculum.

The young people attending this school (aged five to 15) had suffered a range of abuse and neglect. These children found some peace, serenity and improved self-esteem in their lives through our relaxation program. I saw the general school system as a whole failing these children and I wondered why education curricula did not provide 'heart and soul learning' — relaxation and awareness sessions for children of all ages. I am still wondering why this is not happening many years later.

Virginia Field (my long term Tai Chi teacher — 'The Chinese Alchemist' — Blue Mountains, New South Wales) is an inspiration and guide who has encouraged me in my work with young children.

My dear friend Jennifer Sumsion has been an ongoing source of support and encouragement throughout the writing process.

José Pavis, my friend and confidant, through his enthusiasm and creativity has constantly encouraged me because of his belief in me.

My lifelong friends, Karen and Tim Logan and their children Katherine, Mark and Joshua, have provided much love and support during the writing process. These three remarkable children appear throughout the book in photographs and as models for some of the illustrations.

My sister Maureen has been a constant source of support and a 'sounding board' throughout the process.

The material presented in this book has been developed with many groups of children and teachers over the past 20 years — all too numerous to mention. I would like to thank you all for your enthusiasm and interest. In particular, I wish to thank Wendy Shepherd (Director), Jennifer Eaton, Joanne Sykes, Eileen Kalucy and the preschool children from Mia Mia Child and Family Studies Centre at Macquarie University for welcoming me into their setting and working so supportively and creatively with me. I would also like to thank Barbara Raczynsky and her pupils from Kent Road Public School for their enthusiastic support of relaxation and Tai Chi.

I would like to thank my publisher, Rodney Kenner, for having the vision to take this publication on and for his patience and support during some difficult times in bringing the manuscript to fruition.

Finally, I wish to express my gratitude to my partner John, who, from a place of unconditional love and patience, has helped me realise a dream in writing this book.

All of the above people understand the importance of honouring and empowering young children. The ideas presented in this book are a wonderful way to start the journey of self-discovery into 'heart and soul' learning.

Disclaimer

The exercises in this book are gentle and safe provided the instructions are followed carefully. However, the publisher and author disclaim all liability in connection with the use of this information in individual cases. If in doubt, consult your doctor or medical adviser.

Introduction

For many years it has been my dream to write a book about the use of relaxation techniques with young children. This dream emerged from the recognition of the need for children to learn to integrate the physical, mental, emotional and spiritual parts of themselves.

We live in a dramatically changing world and our children are being placed under more and more stress — be it at home, school or in early childhood settings. The importance of developing relaxation techniques for young children is clear (or should be clear to those who love and work with young children).

This book combines gentle exercises (Tai Chi Ch'uan) and progressive relaxation and visualisation techniques that are suitable for all children. Gentle exercise (Tai Chi) promotes strength, flexibility, suppleness, coordination and good posture. Relaxation and visualisation techniques teach children the value of stillness and how to enjoy being calm, quiet and inwardly reflective. Visualisation techniques enhance children's abilities in developing imaginative, creative and artistic habits. Most importantly, relaxation and Tai Chi are non-competitive, nurturing techniques that children of all ages can enjoy.

This guide provides teachers and parents with a starting point for developing their own relaxation programs and home routines for their children. In this way, we can cater for the natural and healthy development of mind, body and spirit.

1
CHAPTER

Transforming Stress in
Young Children

'I like Tai Chi because it's good.' (Boy aged 4 years)

In today's contemporary, fast-paced society, stress is becoming an ever-increasing problem for young children. Stress can have a negative impact upon the health, development and wellbeing of our children. Vast scientific and technological changes have led to a shift in the influences affecting our society. Along with all the benefits the information age has brought, the rapid change has also required the development of special coping skills for adults.

Our children have become the unintended victims of constantly being hurried. We often complete tasks for children (for example, tie their laces, clean up their belongings and their messes and complete chores for them) because it seems more simple and quick for us. By doing this in an ongoing way, we are robbing our children of precious practice in learning life skills and self-esteem. In addition, we are sending the unintentional message of disapproval to them (you take too long to set the table, you don't fold your clothes correctly, it's better if I just do your homework for you, and so on). We all need to learn to be more patient and consistent with our children, by giving them the gift of our time and our belief in their abilities. Hurried parents and teachers produce harried children. Children are often left feeling inadequate, helpless and despondent.

How much daily relaxation time do your children have? A checklist for parents

(This does not mean time in front of the television or computer games!)

It's important for children to have quiet time each day – where they can just "be" – without expectations, noise or activity. Sometimes we push our children too hard and they can suffer from overload.

★ How much time is devoted to relaxation activities for your child each day?

★ Is your child over-scheduled? Extra-curricular activities can be enjoyable and beneficial. However, too many commitments to sport, tutoring, music, dance classes etc can be overwhelming for children.

★ Does your child have difficulty in remembering which activities she/he needs to attend? Has 'looking forward' to an activity been replaced by a feeling of obligation?

★ Is there time for your child to play each day. This does not just mean the very young. All children need to be engaged in fun activities, play, socialising and just 'hanging out' with friends for healthy, balanced development.

★ Does your child have ongoing projects and hobbies at home? Is there a sense of wonder, curiosity and keen problem solving evident in activities around your home?

Many factors contribute to the stresses in young children's lives; these include:

* long hours in child care, school and after school settings;
* spending time with a number of carers;
* being apart from parent/s for much of the day;
* divorce or separation of parents;
* blended families;
* bullying or teasing at school;
* feeling overwhelmed;
* illness;
* financial pressures for parents impacting on children; and
* living at a frantic pace.

In addition, limited space for play and physical development is becoming a feature of Western life. Threats from others prevent children from experiencing free play in parks and gardens. Sedentary lifestyles, 'junk food' diets and the advent of video and computer games for 'relaxation' are further contributors to stress in children.

Western society is slowly coming to understand that health is more than the absence of disease or illness. Health really is about the presence of vitality — the ability to function and live our lives fully, actively, energetically and harmoniously. Harmony and balance have always been central to the Chinese notion of health and wellbeing. Our word 'dis-ease', which means lack of ease, harmony and balance, begins to touch on this notion. Traditionally, Chinese families pay the doctor to keep them well and stop paying when the doctor has to treat them for a sickness. The belief in that philosophy is that the purpose of medicine and doctors is to maintain the balance of the body and harmony of the soul. The practices of **Tai Chi** and relaxation help us to achieve this balance and harmony.

The **YIN YANG** symbol (called 'The Tai Chi') captures the quintessential essence of balance, harmony and equality. Yin and Yang, the opposing forces in each of us (female and male, darkness and light, negative and positive, night and day, death and life, yielding and firm, unconsciousness and consciousness (Galante, 1981, p 29), complement each other in their opposition. Their balance comes from dynamic ongoing tension.

Fundamental to the Chinese worldview, this holding together of opposites has much to offer the West today. It offers a way of understanding the ebbs and flows of our lives — in our relationships, conflicts, work and the surrounding environment — and helps us come to terms with, and have some control over, these forces.

Knowing how to incorporate the benefits of relaxation into daily life provides us with a personal armoury to deal with the unexpected, and often uninvited, intrusions in our lives. Relaxation techniques can be called on in times of trouble, heartache and difficulty.

Tai Chi
The full name is Tai Chi Ch'uan, meaning 'Supreme Ultimate Fist', which refers to the combative martial origins of this exercise. In contemporary times it usually refers to health, relaxation and yin–yang unity.

Yin/Yang
is an ancient Chinese concept that everything is divided into complementary, interdependent opposites.

Chi
means 'energy' or 'life force'.

The Tai-Chi symbol.

This is just as important for children as it is for adults. Through this 'heart and soul' learning, children begin to discover that one of the most interesting worlds to explore is the world inside their heads. Children can be encouraged to discover within themselves a deeper meaning to life.

Real wellness then is:

- ★ physical;
- ★ emotional;
- ★ intellectual;
- ★ spiritual;
- ★ interpersonal;
- ★ social;
- ★ environmental; and
- ★ planetary
    … wellbeing.

We now have far greater control over our health than humans have ever had before — and greater responsibility for it as well. If we take some steps to reduce the everyday risks to our health and that of our children we will be rewarded with:

* higher self-esteem;
* feelings of empowerment;
* a greater sense of control over our lives; and
* more joy in our lives.

Over time we'll come to know, as a way of being:
* greater vitality;
* more energy;
* deeper feelings of curiosity;
* enjoyment;
* interest and enchantment; and
* a higher quality of life.

This list reminds me of the natural state of young children before we impose our stresses and expectations upon them. Pushing our children to achieve too much at an early age can cause them to burn out. Some parents are so keen for their children to live up to their potential that they expect their children to be busy and occupied nearly every waking moment. We all need to find a balance between encouraging our children to experience success in life and allowing them just to be children. Success at school and in other activities is important and worthwhile, but not at the expense of a child's wellbeing and happiness. We need to weave a worldview and develop an ecology of health and wellbeing so that the lives of our children are optimistic and positive, rich in vitality, happiness and fulfilment.

This book takes a holistic, ecological approach to working with children and is based on recognising the following principles in life:

* the value of quiet and solitude;
* the value of **meditation** and reflection (quiet time, prayer, **visualisation**);
* the value of taking care of our bodies;
* the value of intuition, imagination and creativity;
* the awareness of our natural way of being (relaxed and at ease as opposed to feeling stressed);
* the value of ecological awareness and kindness to the earth, its creatures and to each other;
* the value of honest, caring relationships where deep feelings and visions are shared; and
* the value of acknowledging a range of cultures, traditions and rituals.

Visualisation
involves sitting or lying in a still position and imagining a peaceful scene or something we wish to create in our lives.

Hendricks and Wills (1975, p xvii) offered this view:

> It is our belief that a radical change in personal consciousness is necessary to change the course of humanity. We also believe that to open children to see these new ways of seeing the world is to make a loving and profound contribution to the betterment of our world. To expand awareness together with children is liberating, interesting and a great deal of fun.

Meditation
is a standing or sitting practice of experiencing stillness.

This quote was written many years ago and I was heartened and inspired when I read it at the time. Yet, in the ensuing years, little has been done to create programs for children that provide relaxation, self-awareness and relief from stress. Many adults perceive a real gap in our education system. Jenkins (1995, p vii) explains this further:

> As a parent, I feel a great need for more information on mental and spiritual principles in a form easy to share with children.

Much research to date has focused on stress and stress management for adults. However, little focus has been directed at how we can teach holistic stress management skills to children at an early age. Adults often unwittingly transfer their tension and stress reactions to children. It is easy for most adults to verbalise their feelings and begin to take some positive action towards managing their stresses. Children, especially the very young, do not have the words to express their stresses, fears and worries and are often left feeling confused and anxious. Many adults often misinterpret children's stress reactions as inappropriate behaviour. I began learning Tai Chi and relaxation techniques when I began my teaching career in the early 1970s. I sought classes in these techniques for some 'time out', self-nurturing and deeper self-understanding. I wished that someone had taught me these techniques when I was a child.

Learning to relax is a lifelong skill. This book introduces a range of simple techniques that enable children to deal with their stresses more easily.

We can teach children ways to handle stress through gentle exercise and relaxation techniques. These provide children with inner peace, the security of a daily relaxation routine and wellbeing. This guide provides exercises that can easily be used at early childhood centres, schools and homes, with children of most ages.

Gentle exercise for body, mind and spirit

The book concentrates on the gentle exercise of Tai Chi with children, however, many forms of gentle exercise could be substituted. Teachers and parents need to use their discretion and knowledge of their children and the kinds of exercises that are appropriate to different age groups. Here I have focused on simple (and in some cases modified) Tai Chi movements after years of trialling them with a range of age groups across varied settings. The Tai Chi exercises are easy to learn, repetitive and gentle. They also appeal to children's sense of fun and imagination. I have had enormous support for my Tai Chi lessons from early childhood, primary and high school teachers; academics; school counsellors; parents; medical and hospital staff; and especially from the children. Hundreds of people over many years have told me how much they have benefited from the relaxation practices I have shared with them.

Tai Chi and relaxation can be readily integrated into early childhood and school curricula. For example, Tai Chi movements can be used for short transitions or lesson breaks. Tai Chi can also form a strong component of physical education experiences. Physical education and sports in schools are generally geared to performance and competition. Children can be pushed beyond their natural limits and some burn out at an early age. Others damage their young bodies; for example, hip and spine problems may result from some forms of gymnastics and dance. Other, less agile, children can suffer misery and ridicule at being forced to endure team games and sports that they have little natural inclination towards.

Over the years, I have used Tai Chi movements with children with a range of special needs. Children with physical disabilities find that they can do most of the movements and enjoy the feelings of accomplishment that result. Vision and hearing impaired children find Tai Chi movements enjoyable and easy to perform, with little help from an adult needed. Children in wheelchairs can participate in the movements using the upper body and arms. I have conducted Tai Chi and relaxation sessions in hospital rooms with small groups of children and their parents. Some children even participated while sitting up in bed!

In our rich, diverse, multicultural society, Tai Chi is one form of move-ment and exercise that acknowledges the traditions of an Asian culture. One Asian parent (having just arrived in Sydney) told me how pleased she and her husband were to hear that their daughter would be learning Tai Chi in the preschool class where I was helping out. The mother explained how important it was for her daughter to experience a familiar and loved practice from her birth country. The practice helps to enrich all our lives.

Tai Chi, visualisation and meditation are now no longer as feared as they were, even 10 years ago, as 'New Age' or religious. They are mainstream practices for adults in our contemporary, multicultural society. But what about children? They also need to find their own inner peace and contentment — independent of the people and situations around them.

Relaxation and visualisation sessions can also be incorporated into the creative arts and serve as innovative ways to explore drama, story telling, writing and art experiences. Ideally, a Tai Chi and relaxation session takes place for at least 20 minutes per day. Parents can use Tai Chi and relaxation exercises at home with the whole family as a way of coming together and positively working on stress and tiredness. It may also be used for exercise and enjoyment and it is a fun way of keeping the 'lines of communication' open between children and parents. The creative visu-alisation scripts are especially useful at bedtime to ensure a peaceful night's sleep.

Tai Chi and relaxation will not appeal to everyone — adults and children alike. Therefore, like any activity, it is worth giving it a try and experi-encing its benefits — there is nothing to lose by doing this. If children do not feel comfortable in undertaking any of these exercises, allow them to sit and watch or engage in an alternative activity whilst other children are participating in it.

How relaxation helps children

★ Relaxes the body

★ Quietens the mind

★ Allows the child to simply 'be'

★ Provides rest and rejuvenation

★ Opens the children's imagination and creativity

★ Allows children to 'feel good' about themselves

★ Provides 'time-out' and solitude

★ Helps coping skills

★ Develops self-awareness

★ Provides enjoyable, uplifting experiences

(Rickard, J., 1994; Thomas, P. and Shepherd, W., 2000)

Ask yourself: How can I develop an ecology of relaxation in my life?

Before embarking on a relaxation program with your children, it is important to ensure that relaxation is a part of your life already. This means integrating relaxation as a 'way of being' in our lives rather than just seeing it as another technique that can be used to 'fix' ourselves and children when stress becomes too much. Many educators and parents want their children to learn to relax but often fail to see how their own stressful behaviours impact upon those around them. The following ideas outline ways that we can develop an ecology of relaxation.

Personal ... develop a 'relaxed way of being'

There are personal areas you can work on to develop a relaxed way of being. We need to acknowledge each of these areas throughout the day — whether at work or at home. These include your breath, voice, posture, language, empathy, philosophy and commitment.

Breath

Breath is intrinsically linked with relaxation — a raced breath often equals a raced mind. Continually remind yourself to return to relaxed and comfortable breathing throughout the day.

Voice

Voice is another indicator of either a calm or uptight state. Often we do not realise that we speak too quickly or too loudly much of the time. Notice whether your voice is calm and relaxed or whether it is 'jarring' to those around you. Work on developing a calm, even speaking voice.

Posture
Good/correct posture alleviates muscular strain. Developing a comfortable, aligned posture will help you move through the day with more ease and confidence.

Language
Negative language causes disharmony and tension. Try to eliminate the language of negativity, judgment and criticism from your vocabulary. Use the language of encouragement and optimism around children.

Empathy
Showing care, consideration, thoughtfulness and kindness to others reaps its own rewards. Model tolerant and respectful behaviour to those around you.

Philosophy
We can develop a personal and professional philosophy around relaxation and self-awareness skills. Sometimes we sabotage our intentions to introduce positive changes into our daily lives by saying one thing and then doing the opposite. We all need to commit to a philosophy of relaxation that integrates all areas of our lives.

Commitment
Making a heart and soul commitment to relaxation will help ensure that it becomes a much loved and enjoyed part of our overall approach to life.

Transforming stress into vitality

Relaxation techniques can transform stress into vitality when practised on a daily basis. Try to incorporate some of the following ideas into your daily routines.

Breathing techniques
Relaxation research (Farhi, 1997) shows that breathing techniques are the most readily accessible resource we have for creating and sustaining our vital energy. Breathing practice can help ward off disease by increasing our immune system's functioning and by lowering blood pressure and cholesterol levels.

Meditation, prayer and reflection
Insight and connection to intuition (inner knowing; soul self) can be developed through the regular practise of a meditative discipline such as prayer, reflection and visualisation. Through these practices we can tap into the power, richness and creativity of our inner world.

Exercise
Exercise (for example, Tai Chi, yoga, walking, swimming, gardening) practised for at least 20 minutes on three days per week relaxes our bodies and minds. Exercise helps to burn off 'stress chemicals' that can accumulate in our bodies. Regular breaks for walking, moving or stretching throughout the day are also beneficial.

Goals
Setting goals that are in tune with your ecology of relaxation will help to lessen the effects of stress and provide tangible direction for your aims to become fit, relaxed and healthy.

Good nutrition
A healthy, balanced diet consisting of fresh food helps your body combat the toll that stress can take. Consult a physician or dietician or simply buy some books on good nutrition to put good eating habits in place. Avoid resorting to convenience 'junk' foods when experiencing stress.

Drinking sufficient water
Drinking clean, purified water enhances many bodily functions, including the way you react to stress. Lethargy and fatigue often result from too little water consumption. Hydration, or adding more water to your diet, assists in maintaining calm feelings as well as preventing many health problems (for example, constipation, headache and hypertension).

Positive time management
Positive time management helps us achieve our goals and manage ourselves in a calm and productive way. Stress is often caused when we 'manage by crisis'. Relaxed people plan their days so that they are not burdened by inflexible deadlines and relentless schedules. Taking time out for ourselves to relax and refresh each day is important.

Relaxation
The ongoing practise of relaxation exercises such as those presented throughout the book (progressive muscle relaxation, for example) can bring peace and contentment into our lives. You can practise these alone, by listening to a tape, or join a group.

Sacred time
Part of bringing a calm way of being into your life is to provide sacred time and space for yourself. Spending time alone, surrounded by objects that enhance the atmosphere of relaxation (candles, flowers, quiet music) helps us nourish ourselves and 'fill the well' before it becomes too depleted. Set aside a relaxation space in your home and spend time alone there each day if possible.

Positive affirmations
Affirmations can help you achieve your aspirations in life. Affirmation (or auto-suggestion) is a technique that involves the repetition of carefully chosen words or sentiments. We can achieve the results we desire in life (both immediate and long term) and change unproductive habits and stress responses. The repetition of positive statements or affirmations influences the subconscious and becomes self-fulfilling. For example:
'I am now calm and relaxed.'
'I now eat healthy, fresh food every day.'
'I am a creative and talented person.'
'I exercise three times a week to keep my body and mind in good shape.'
'I am organised and efficient at work.'

Self-nurturing

Self-nurturing is an essential part of transforming stress and bringing happiness and calm into your life. Explore ways to de-stress during the day (for example, a warm bath with fragrant oil and candles at the end of a busy day).

Work environment

We can also learn to transform stress in the work environment. Try to include some of the following suggestions for developing a more relaxed 'way of being'.

Uncluttered work stations

Remove all clutter from work stations and other areas. Clutter creates disorganisation and mental confusion. Organised, tidy work stations help us to achieve our goals and efficiently attend to the tasks at hand.

Be organised

Try to spend a few minutes each morning to plan your day and set priorities. In this time, you can organise your desk, set the day's objectives and gather your thoughts. Deep breathing exercises are also useful at this point.

Functional and comfortable furnishings

Include a balance of functional as well as comfortable furnishings in your work environment. This is especially important if you work with children. As well as the necessary desks, shelves, cupboards and filing cabinets, introduce soft, aesthetically pleasing furniture items. These can include lounge chairs, cushions, soft fabrics and hangings and any other elements that bring a relaxing feel to the indoor environment.

Workable systems

Ensure that your work routines are efficient and help you achieve your relaxation goals. Investigate some of your age-old work habits and routines. It may be time to replace these with more workable ones. For example, persisting with 'sleep time' for all children in a preschool group as the year progresses can often cause more problems than benefits. Try a relaxation and visualisation session instead.

Aesthetically pleasing decorating items

Introduce aesthetically pleasing decorating items. We can bring a stale environment alive with beautiful objects from home. Simple additions, such as a vase of fresh flowers or light, flowing curtains or hangings, can lift our spirits on busy, tiring work days.

Hang posters

Bring environmental posters into the workplace. Unless we work directly with children, we may not find an opportunity to enjoy a visualisation exercise during the day. We can, however, bring posters and prints for example, rainforest, beach, mountains, desert etc) that remind us of the restful and healing power of nature.

Crystals

Crystals, gemstones and rocks can bring feelings of restfulness and relaxation into work and home environments. Quartz crystal is a powerful tool for use in energising and protecting areas at work and home. Gemstones and rocks bring elements of nature into otherwise sterile work environments.

Windchimes

Windchimes invite 'the spirit of the wind' into our surroundings. Windchimes soothe the soul and are said to protect and heal the buildings where they are placed. A gentle breeze or a light touch can bring forth their delicate sound.

Aromatherapy

Aromatherapy techniques, such as using oil burners, fragrant sprays and essential oils, can heal the body, uplift emotions and relieve tension (Nagy, 1995). Do not leave a naked candle flame burning near children. It is also important to be aware of the contraindications for some essential oils; for example, do not use clary sage and some other oils during pregnancy.

Plants/flowers

Bringing plants and flowers indoors transmits the tranquility of the natural world. When we contemplate the colours, textures, fragrances and shapes of plants and flowers we relax the tight focus that life often imposes upon us.

Drink water

Place a jug of clean water on your desk. Drinking sufficient water keeps our bodies hydrated and cleanses our bodily systems.

Drink herbal tea

Replace caffeine drinks, such as tea, coffee and cola, with herbal teas during the day. For example, chamomile tea is now a widely accepted calming drink. Peppermint tea has cleansing and calming properties. Dandelion root is a good coffee substitute and is useful in the treatment of anxiety. Chai is a popular Indian drink and has calming, relaxing properties. Add honey or a slice of lemon to herbal teas to make them more appealing.

Play music

Play quiet, relaxing music in the background in your work environment. Music can have a profound effect on lessening our feelings of stress and anxiety. The ideal relaxation music has a slow tempo and rhythm; for example, ambient, instrumental and slow baroque pieces. Experiment with music that your colleagues will enjoy and build on your collection of CDs/tapes over time. Children will especially enjoy hearing a variety of music during their day.

Take breaks

Take short breaks during the day to breathe deeply, stretch, revive and replenish. Stretching exercises at your office desk, a Tai Chi exercise or a short walk will energise your body and lift your spirit.

Reward yourself

Provide yourself with small treats and rewards occasionally. For example, meet a friend in a café after completing a big work assignment or book an aromatherapy massage once a month as a 'treat'.

When your are working — work

When you are working — work; and when you are relaxing — relax. Often the 'lines are blurred' between work and relaxation time. Sometimes we waste valuable work time by daydreaming and wishing we were relaxing in the outdoors. This results in loss of productive time and unfinished tasks. Conversely, some people never 'turn off', even when they think they are relaxing. For example, worrying about a deadline during a brisk walk on the weekend will defeat the purpose of this relaxation pursuit. Try to create a positive balance between work and relaxation in your life.

Communicate

Communicate your needs to the people around you. Feelings of stress often arise when we fail to state our needs directly and assertively. If you require uninterrupted time during the day for important tasks, you need to tell those around you. Try to negotiate a balance at work so that everyone's needs can be acknowledged.

Make technology work for you

In these days of 'labour saving devices', such as telephones, faxes and computers, we are often bombarded with technological overload. Make your telephone 'work for you' by installing an answering machine or voicemail so that your day is not consumed in answering calls. Develop workable systems that fit in well with your ecology of relaxation.

An over-riding philosophy

Develop an over-riding philosophy in your life. Regard relaxation as a way of being rather than something that we do to ourselves and others. *It is a way of transforming stress and anxiety in life through a relaxed, gentle, calm, life-enhancing approach to living.*

Incorporating the above holistic suggestions on a daily basis will help you to be more relaxed in all areas of your life. The aim is to implement relaxation practices in your life's philosophy and enjoy participating in these each day. In this way, we have the skills and self-understanding to deal with stressful situations when they arise.

Note: These ideas are not meant to be prescriptive but to serve to clarify our motivations for wanting to introduce relaxation into the lives of our children.

Getting Started

'Me painting the rainbow.' (Boy aged 4 years)

How to begin

Provide a quiet place

The room or space you use for relaxation should be large enough for all children to lie on the floor without touching each other. The area needs to be clean, warm, carpeted, away from noise and 'traffic' areas and, if possible, have soft lighting such as lamps.

Set the scene

The children can help you 'dress the room' or area used for relaxation as part of their daily activities. For example, have posters of scenes from nature on the walls and include children's drawings showing their impressions of their relaxation journeys. Decorate the area with pot plants, flowers and mobiles. Have a relaxation or awareness book corner and provide cushions for when individuals or small groups of children want to spend time in the area apart from designated relaxation sessions. A fish tank, candles, soft and exotic draping materials and relaxing music all add to the ambience of your special relaxation space. Aesthetics are important to a relaxing experience.

Use candles, flowers, bells or ornaments to create a centrepiece for your relaxation circle.

Music

There are some excellent compact discs and tapes available for relaxation with adults and children. Browse your local ABC or music shop and seek out ambient music with rainforest, beach, bird, dolphin or other relaxing themes. Play this music at other times of the day to signal the need for calm, quiet activity. It will help children become more relaxed and at ease during the day.

Entering the relaxation space

Start with an attitude of reverence and respect for the relaxation space you and the children have created together. Have the children remove their shoes but keeps socks on. No special clothing is required but, in winter, children might need a small mat to lie on and a rug to cover them whilst they are doing their relaxation.

Routine and ritual

Behaviour problems should not arise if you talk to the children about what you will all be doing in the relaxation area. Explain why you are doing Tai Chi and relaxation and how it can help. Set up expectations for this area just as you would in any other activity. For example, stress the need to listen and pay attention, not to touch others and to lie still during relaxations. Some young children enjoy holding a teddy bear ('relaxation bear') while they are lying down for **progressive relaxation** time. Stroking the bear can be soothing and calming.

Progressive relaxation involves sitting or lying still and relaxing each of the body parts with the breath in sequence.

A preschool boy loves holding 'relaxation teddy' during our sessions.

A greeting and goodbye ritual is useful and engages the children's interest. One derived from Tai Chi practice is:

'Form a fist with your right hand. This is your sun. Then place your left hand around your fist. This is your moon. Raise your sun/moon to your forehead and bow slightly. This is a ritual of respect and reverence.'

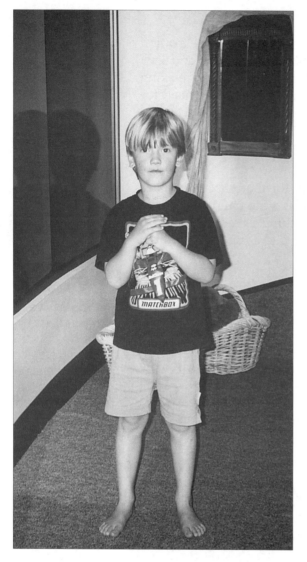

A preschool boy is preparing his 'sun and moon' actions to make a bow.

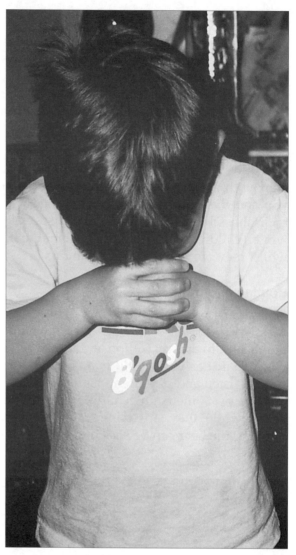

Making the ritual bow before and after Tai Chi exercise.

One key to successful relaxation sessions with children is the development of a routine. Choose a 'relaxation time' and stick to it each day. Ensure that the children know what they need to do on entering and leaving the space. If not, provide a gentle reminder of your expectations. Do not proceed with the Tai Chi or relaxation unless the children are ready to listen.

The educator's/parent's role

The educator's/parent's role is one of leader and participant. It is helpful if other available adults share relaxation time as well (student teachers, assistants, parents, even invite the director or school principal to join in!). You are the model and guide for the children. They will reflect your attitudes to the relaxation sessions. Too many times I have seen staff stand on the sidelines (some even chatting away), fully expecting the children to learn to relax but giving no thought to their own tense and off-putting behaviour. We are fortunate in centres and schools as we can actually put our stress management ideas into practice on a daily basis with our children. It is not so easy if we work in a shop or a bank! It is vitally important for you to share your responses to the Tai Chi exercises and to talk about your feelings and experiences after the relaxation sessions with the children as well as expecting them to listen and share. It is YOUR attitude and approach to all aspects of relaxation that will 'make or break' the program.

Important teacher qualities

It is important for teachers to model the qualities of relaxation to those around them. Ensure that you acknowledge the points outlined below.

Calm and reassuring voice

The tone of your voice is important. Keep it firm but not overly loud. Speak naturally but evenly and slowly. Use expression and voice intonation to emphasise words. You may need to repeat key words or phrases a couple of times. Remember — slow … clear … calm.

Encouragement

Much of what you do in relaxation may be new for some children. Sharing feelings always involves risk-taking for children. Your willingness to share with children, accept all of their responses and encourage them to participate, is vital.

Acceptance

We all respond to and experience relaxation in different ways. Some people actually 'see' the images being described to them, whilst others have vague images or impressions of the spoken words. Other people can actually sense, smell and hear the things that are being described. Others still cannot 'visualise' at all but enjoy the light and the sensations they feel when they are relaxing. No two children will have exactly the same experience in relaxation sessions. It is important for the teacher/parent to accept and affirm the offerings and responses children make to the relaxation techniques. If any 'silliness' arises, simply outline your expectations again and redirect the children's attention to a key word or to a comment offered by another child. You will find that relaxation time becomes 'cherished' by the children and that any off-putting behaviour quickly diminishes.

Remember — be clear, be firm and be consistent!

Feedback and positive reinforcement

Children need affirmation and encouragement throughout the relaxation session. Ensure that you genuinely and warmly provide children with 'positives' and reassuring feedback throughout the exercises, the progressive relaxation and visualisation time and in the follow-up group discussion.

Kindergarten children enjoy learning Tai Chi — this movement is called 'The Bird'.

Structure of the relaxation session

As you become more comfortable and familiar with using relaxation in your setting, you will begin to structure your relaxation sessions specifically for the needs of your children. An overall guide is set out below and includes the following:

★ beginning circle;
★ Tai Chi exercises;
★ progressive relaxation and visualisation; and
★ a sharing circle.

Beginning circle

Have children enter the space and form a circle. Use the Tai Chi greeting (sun and moon) and bow. Then ask the children to sit on the floor and BRIEFLY explain what they will be doing. A few seconds with eyes closed and focusing on breathing will 'centre' the group. Focusing on a candle or a float bowl with flowers helps set the scene.

Tai Chi exercises

Have the children stand up and quietly find their own space, facing you. Tai Chi movements help children learn to move in a relaxed way. Begin the Tai Chi exercises slowly. Teach two or three new exercises each week. Review what you have learned each day until you have built up a Tai Chi routine.

If children become restless, do a stretch (hands above heads; breathe in, bend down; touch floor; breathe out) and then remind them of your expectations *(see Chapter 3).*

Progressive relaxation and visualisation

Ask children to lie down on the carpet on their backs with their legs and arms relaxed and their eyes closed. (This can be threatening for some children so gently encourage them to shut their eyes a little at a time and gradually lengthen the time the eyes are closed.)

Read the script for the progressive relaxation and breathing. You will quickly develop your own style and rhythm for this and will not be reliant on actually 'reading' it for more than a couple of weeks. When all body parts have been relaxed, begin reading a visualisation script *(see Chapter 4).*

Always bring children out of a visualisation/relaxation exercise slowly and respectfully. Do not ask them to open their eyes and stand up too quickly. The children need to reorient and 'earth' themselves. If children are a little slow or tired after relaxation, do a couple of standing stretches or waist swings to re-energise them.

Sharing circle

Have the children hold hands and 'feel the magic' of the relaxation and energy they have created. A 'trick' that children love is to rub their hands together and hold them up in the air to 'catch the magic' in the room. Do this three or four times, and tell them to stroke their tingling hands over their faces, arms, legs etc.

Now share a few responses and reactions to the relaxation session. Some children will want to talk about their Tai Chi, some will want to talk about their 'journey' and some will not want to share their experiences at all.

Make a point of asking each child how they are and what their experiences were like. This section of the session can be followed up by painting, drawing, modelling, patterning or creative movement activities. For example, if children have done a visualisation on 'A Walk in the Rainforest', they may want to paint or draw what they felt, saw, heard, smelled and so on.

Feeling the Magic.

Preschoolers preparing to share visualisation experiences in a talking circle.

Managing children's behaviour

It is not the purpose of this book to outline a range of methods for managing the 'inappropriate' and at times troubling behaviour of children. There is a wealth of texts on this subject.

However, I strongly believe that the incorporation of an 'ecology of relaxation' into early childhood centres and schools as well as into children's homes will serve as a preventative measure against many 'discipline' problems highlighted by educators and parents alike.

Relaxation sessions are not a blanket solution to the many educational, health and behavioural difficulties experienced by our children in today's society — they are not intended to be. These sessions do, however, provide an alternative way of working with children that honours their individuality and their needs for respect, inclusion in decision making and acknowledgment of their inner lives.

Events that represent change in children's lives can cause them stress. These may include:

★ loss of a parent, relative, friend or even a pet through death;
★ separation or divorce of parents;
★ the addition of a new baby to the family;
★ moving house;
★ bullying or teasing at school;
★ abuse and neglect;
★ family violence;

★ learning difficulties;
★ illness or hospitalisation;
★ excessive expectations from families;
★ disability; and
★ cultural isolation.

Children react to stress and change in many ways (aggression, with-drawal, attention seeking, disobedience, difficulty sleeping or eating, bed wetting, irritability, sadness or tearfulness, changes in toileting habits and bullying others as well as physical symptoms such as headaches or stomach aches). Some of these reactions are interpreted as misbehaviour or 'inappropriate behaviour'.

We can help children learn to recognise stress and how their bodies and minds react to it. This can be done with young children right through to teenagers. Children can learn to recognise when they are feeling angry, sad, upset, tired and annoyed, and the accompanying body signals. Once they have learned some ways to use relaxation to help them with these symptoms and feelings, they can begin to see the benefits of the techniques and will want to keep using them. In this way, we can teach children life-long methods of coping with the difficult situations that life presents to them.

All too often, we label children with disorders such as 'ADHD' or 'hyper-active'. I am not suggesting that difficulties with behaviour and attention do not exist. After all, I have been teaching in regular and special schools for many years and I have seen a wide range of behaviours and syndromes. I am, however, concerned with the recent trend of medicating or 'drugging' our children to slow them down and 'control' their behaviour to make them more compliant. Prescribing drugs to manage children's behaviour is often done as a 'first resort' rather than exploring more natural methods. Perhaps the prescription of medication is a simplistic answer to the problems of a complex world. Are we teaching our children that problems can be 'fixed' with drugs? How can we then help them to understand the dangers of addictive substances that create dependency and a plethora of other social and moral issues? I believe that we should be empowering our children by offering them choices and alternatives in managing their lives and solving their problems. In order to create optimistic and well balanced children, we need to teach them life skills that touch their hearts and their souls as well as their bodies and their minds. For too long, schools have been focusing on physical and intellectual development at the expense of the 'whole' child (namely the spiritual person inside each of us). We owe it to our children to at least explore the potential of a relaxation program as one way of working with them.

Relaxation skills take time to develop. We need to introduce the techniques offered in this book slowly and sensitively. A relaxation program at home or at school does not represent a 'quick fix' method — nor does it aim to do so. Relaxation is a life skill that provides children and adults with an approach for coping with the unexpected and often stressful circumstances that present themselves. At the very least, we could begin to use relaxation techniques alongside medication so that children learn self-coping and self-soothing skills as well as being 'slowed down' by chemical, external means.

A relaxation program provides a very special, nurturing time for partici- pating adults and children alike. Children quickly learn to cherish and look forward to their relaxation sessions. Relaxation time can create bonds of understanding and friendship because it allows children to simply 'be' — children appreciate and accept this. Listening skills, turn taking, respect and sensitive communication can all be enhanced through the development of the activities outlined in the program. Creativity and self-expression are natural outcomes of relaxation and visualisation sessions.

Relaxation sessions are not expensive (they're free!), they cannot harm children and they do not involve complicated behaviour management or drug therapy programs. Surely relaxation is worth a try … we have nothing to lose and everything to gain!

Clearly, children who are very stressed or sick need more help than educators or parents can provide. When children's stress levels are chronic and on-going, it is best to refer them to a medical doctor and/or a school counsellor, paediatrician, psychologist or other professional. Educators, parents, medical and welfare professionals can work together to help children regain their balance and healthy outlook on life. Children may need extra help when they:

Children are content and joyful after their relaxation sessions.

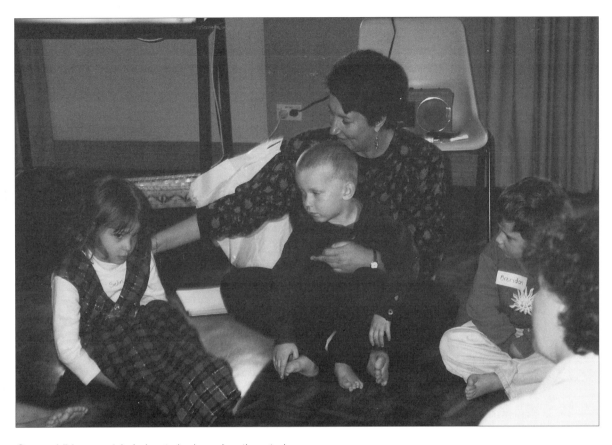

Some children are 'shy' about sharing relaxation stories.

★ are overly lethargic or depressed;

★ seem to be more and more sad and are crying often;

★ are increasingly aggressive;

★ are experiencing ongoing eating problems;

★ are suffering from fears and phobias that limit their everyday enjoyment of life;

★ are increasingly unable to concentrate on school tasks; or

★ seem to be overly withdrawn.

Helping parents to introduce relaxation techniques at home

Parents want what is best for their children, but often need guidance and support from teachers when trying different strategies. Bennett (1996, p 16) notes that:

> *Children who use visualization regularly tend to be healthy with a keen concentration, and the ability to take responsibility for their actions. They become very creative.*

The success of a school relaxation program can be enhanced when it is supported and used by parents at home (and vice versa).

It is important for teachers to communicate with parents throughout the planning and implementation stages of the relaxation program. This two-way communication will lead to shared ideas, resources and experiences. In this way, parents and teachers can work collaboratively on 'tailoring' the relaxation program to suit the children's needs.

Parents often ask for help and ideas when they want their children to:

* learn to slow down;
* develop concentration;
* fall to sleep easily;
* experience contentment; and
* connect with their inner selves.

Teachers can guide parents through the following useful steps when they are embarking on relaxation time at home. Many of these ideas are similar to earlier suggestions provided for setting up a school relaxation program. Parents can adapt these ideas to suit their children's needs.

Beginning 'relaxation time' at home

* Choose a corner (or a spare room) that can become the family 'relaxation space'.

* Decorate the area with relaxing posters, mobiles, hangings, soft cushions, lamps, flowers, plants, a 'relaxation teddy' and other mood creating objects.

* Use aromatherapy (for example, an oil burner) and ambient music to set the scene.

* Ask the children what they would like to achieve in their relaxation times at home. Ask them how this can be achieved best.

* Set some ground rules for relaxation time. This time should be respected by all participants and, as such, courtesies such as listening, caring for others, using quiet voices, taking turns with siblings and so on, should be observed.

* Choose a 'relaxation time' to suit family members who wish to participate; for example, on arrival home after preschool/school or before bed time. Some families have a Tai Chi time in the early evening where they perform some exercises together and then sit quietly on the floor or chairs for a short meditation. Where bedtime is a problem for families, breathing and visualisation techniques are shared with children before they drift off to sleep.

* Follow the guidelines set out in this book for Tai Chi, progressive relaxation and visualisation exercises. Experiment with the ideas offered and add your own.

* Complete your relaxation sessions with a short discussion in the same way teachers do in the centre or school. Family members can share their experiences and feelings and describe what they saw or 'visualised' during the process. This is an empowering and respectful way to bring closure to the relaxation process.

Running Head

3

CHAPTER

Gentle Tai Chi Exercises

'Happy.' (Girl aged 6 years)

Warm up exercises

As with other forms of exercise, it is important to warm up the muscles, ligaments and joints of the body in preparation for Tai Chi movements. This can be done by performing simple limbering and stretching movements with the children. These warm ups are not prescriptive and you can include any favourites you already use with your children.

These exercises can be used in a modified way with children with mobility problems and other physical needs.

Cleansing breath

★ Have the children find their own space and stand with their feet at about shoulder width apart.

★ Bend knees slightly and sink down a little.

★ Ask the children to breathe in and stretch their arms up over their heads (see Warm up Figure 1(a)).

★ Now, as the children breathe out, ask them to bend forward, trying to bring their hands down to touch their feet — without bending the knees too much! (see Warm up Figure 1(b)). Return to the position in Warm up Figure 1(a).

★ Repeat this exercise a few times.

Warm up 1(a)   Warm up 1(b)

Stretching the arms

★ Ask the children to stand with their feet shoulder width apart and hold their arms bent at shoulder height with palms facing outwards (see Warm up Figure 2(a)).

★ Without moving the body, push the palms out to the side, as if pushing against a wall (see Warm up Figure 2(b)).

★ Return to the position in Warm up Figure 2(a)

★ Repeat this exercise several times, adding variations if you wish (for example, hands reaching forward etc).

Warm up 2(a)   Warm up 2(b)

Waist swings

★ Ask the children to stand with their feet shoulder width apart holding their arms stretched out to their sides at waist height with palms down, breathing in (see Warm up Figure 3(a)).

★ Rotate the body around to the right side, breathe out and face the back wall, keeping the arms out to the side and the feet 'glued' to the floor.

★ Now swing slowly around through the front (breathe in) and around to the left side.

★ Look around to the back wall, breathing out as you turn your body (see Warm up Figure 3(b)).

★ Repeat this exercise several times.

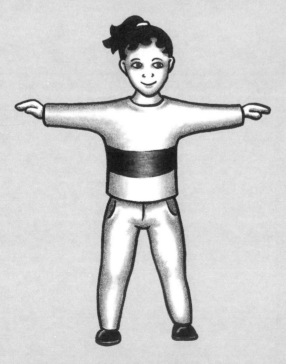

Warm up 3(a)

Warm up 3(b)

Tai Chi movements

Tai Chi Ch'uan (or Tai Chi) is an ancient form of Chinese exercise and soft martial art dating back hundreds of years. Tai Chi or 'Supreme Ultimate' is derived from Taoist principles and relates to the 'yin and yang' of all life being harmoniously interconnected.

Tai Chi exercises are beneficial for the mind, body and spirit and, as such, are excellent for children and adults alike. When we perform these movements we are activating our **chi** or life force. The slow movements accompanied with rhythmical breathing enhance health, coordination and flexibility. The 'moving meditation' principles of Tai Chi create feelings of peace, harmony, calm, quiet and happiness in children. Tai Chi also promotes good posture, muscle tone and suppleness. I have participated in and 'played' Tai Chi with children as young as two years of age (in a modified form), through to primary and secondary school students. They love the repetitive, flowing movements and relate easily to the symbolism expressed in the names of the movements.

Chi
means 'energy' or 'life force'.

Tai Chi brings the body back into its natural balance. In urban, Western society, physical exercise is no longer a part of everyday life for children (or adults!). Whilst other forms of exercise (gymnastics, aerobics) can be useful, they often do not work on the joints, nor do they integrate the mind, body and spirit. Growing bodies require lots of movement opportunities to help them develop. Traditional exercises and sports can be helpful for many children, however, inappropriate exercise and too much competitive sport can be damaging. It is vital, therefore, to introduce children to gentle, non-invasive exercise in order to develop a healthy, balanced lifestyle before negative habits set in.

I have developed the following sequence of Tai Chi movements for children, to be undertaken before progressive relaxation and visualisation exercises. I believe that before the mind can relax, the body must learn to relax. This idea seems to be a missing element in most relaxation programs. Tai Chi gently prepares the body and the mind to become still, calm and relaxed.

Tai Chi is a gentle, non-competitive, peaceful form of exercise. I have taught Tai Chi in early childhood centres, preschools, schools and in hospital settings. Children of all ages can benefit from Tai Chi in terms of their physical, mental, emotional and spiritual development. Children often tell me how much they enjoy hearing the names of the different movements. Some alternative names are included in brackets beside the conventional names. Repeat each movement one to eight times depending on the age of the children and the stage through which they are progressing with their Tai Chi. Begin by introducing only two or three movements and gradually build up to the whole set of movements over time.

Let us now begin our Tai Chi with a bow making a 'sun and moon' with our hands (see page 18). Always begin your Tai Chi sessions with warm up exercises, such as limbering or stretching. In this way, the children's muscles, ligaments and joints will be prepared for the Tai Chi movements that follow.

Movement 1: Wu Chi (Raising the arms)

★ Place your feet shoulder width apart.

★ Slightly bend your knees and sink down a little. This is commonly known as the 'Horse Riding Stance'. Breathe in and out naturally. Keep your spine straight. It is important to commit this movement to memory as most Tai Chi movements start from this stance (see Figure 1-A).

★ Stand with your feet almost parallel.

★ Raise both your arms to shoulder height in front of you, shoulder width apart with palms facing down. Breathe in as you do this and imagine your arms floating up to shoulder height like balloons (see Figures 1-B and 1-C).

★ Slowly move your palms down until your hands are by your sides again. Breathe out as you do this.

★ Slightly bend your knees as you lower your arms (see Figure 1-A).

★ Repeat this movement a few times.

Figure 1-A

Preparing for Wu Chi in the Horse Riding Stance.

Figure 1-B

Imagine your arms floating up to shoulder height like balloons.

Figure 1-C

Slowly move your arms down towards your sides.

Movement 2: Expanding the heart (Wu Chi 2)

★ Begin in the Horse Riding Stance. Breathe naturally. Hold a comfortable posture.

★ Raise both arms to shoulder height in front of you with palms facing down.

★ As in Wu Chi, imagine your arms floating up like balloons (see Figure 2-A).

★ As you breathe out, extend your arms out to the sides at shoulder height (see Figure 2-B).

★ Breathe in and return to position illustrated in Figure 2-A.

★ Return to the Horse Riding Stance.

★ Repeat this movement a few times.

Figure 2-A

As you breathe out, begin to extend your arms to the sides.

Figure 2-B

Extend your arms outwards as you breathe out.

Movement 3: Holding up heaven (Holding up the clouds)

★ Begin in the Horse Riding Stance (see Figure 3-A).

★ Link fingers with palms facing upwards.

★ Inhaling, draw the palms slowly upwards at the same time rising on to the balls of the feet (see Figure 3-B).

★ Turn the palms over when they reach chest height (see Figure 3-C).

★ Still inhaling, continue to press the palms upward whilst fully stretching the body towards 'heaven'.

★ Follow the hands with your gaze (see Figures 3-D and 3-E).

★ Hold the inhalation for about three counts and then slowly exhale, gradually reversing the order of the movements.

★ Remember to turn the palms back over at chest height.

★ Complete the movement and exhalation at the beginning posture (back to Figure 3-A).

Figure 3-A

Begin in the Horse Riding Stance.

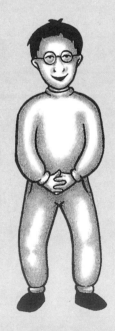

Figure 3-B

Link your fingers, with the palms facing upwards.

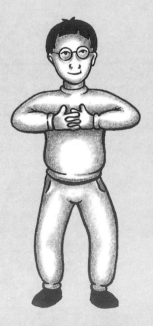

Figure 3-C

Draw the palms slowly up to the chest height.

Figure 3-D

Turn the palms outward as you
continue to raise your arms.

Figure 3-E

Extend the linked hands
above your head.

Movement 4: Turning the waist and pushing the palm (Tying a bow)

★ Begin in the Horse Riding Stance (see Figure 4-A).

★ Keeping the feet firmly on the ground begin to turn the waist 45 degrees to the left as you inhale.

★ At the same time, bring your right hand, palm up, across your body at chest height.

★ As you exhale push your right hand out behind you as your turn further around to the left.

★ Keep your left palm turned over beside you and press it down beside your left thigh (see Figure 4-B).

★ Return to the Horse Riding Stance.

★ Repeat the movement.

★ Inhale, this time turning the body 45 degrees to the right, pushing out around and behind you with the left palm facing up and then out as you exhale (see Figure 4-C).

★ Return to the Horse Riding Stance.

★ Repeat the movement to alternate sides several times.

Figure 4-A

Begin in the Horse Riding Stance.

Figure 4-B

Exhale as you push your right hand out behind you. Turn your body to the left as you do this.

Figure 4-C

Repeat using the left hand and turning your body to the right.

Movement 5: Painting a rainbow (Dancing rainbows)

★ Begin in the Horse Riding Stance (see Figure 5-A).

★ Raise your hands in front of your body and take them over your head.

★ Shift body weight to the right side.

★ Bend the right knee and at the same time curve the right palm over the head so that it faces the top of your head, then inhale. The elbow is relaxed in a gentle curve.

★ Simultaneously, lower the left arm to shoulder height on the left side of the body, turning the body slightly to the left to look out at the left palm. Exhale (see Figure 5-B).

★ Reverse arms by repeating the movements to the other side.

★ Raise the left hand up over the head so the palm faces the top of the head.

★ Weight is on the left leg with the left knee bent. Inhale.

★ Simultaneously, lower right arm to shoulder height on the right side of the body.

★ Palm up, turn the body to the right, look at right palm. Exhale (see Figure 5-C).

★ Repeat movement on alternating sides several times.

Figure 5-A

Begin in the Horse Riding Stance, then raise your arms above your head.

Figure 5-B

Curve the right palm over your head and lower your left arm out to the side.

Figure 5-C

Change arms. repeat the movement by curving the left arm over your head and lowering your right arm out to the side.

Movement 6: Punching in a Horse Riding Stance (Star fists)

★ Begin in the Horse Riding Stance.

★ Draw hands into fists, bend elbows and raise the hands to the side of the waist, knuckles facing down. Inhale (see Figure 6-A).

★ As you punch forward with the right fist, twist it over, so the knuckles face up at chest height. Exhale (see Figure 6-B).

★ Draw the fist back down to the side of your waist, rotating the wrist to bring the knuckles back to the starting position (see Figure 6-A).

★ Repeat the movement using the left hand (see Figure 6-C).

★ Repeat this movement several times.

★ This is a martial arts movement and it should be stressed to the children that we never use our fists (or any part of our bodies) to hurt another person. This movement can help children to relieve their stress.

★ The preschoolers I worked with called this movement 'Star Fists' as they liked to release the outward punch and extend their fingers out like stars.

★ Imagine that you are punching away any anger, worry, tiredness, silliness or wriggles as you do this movement.

Figure 6-A

Draw hands into fists and raise them to waist height.

Figure 6-B

Punch forward—slowly—with the right fist, turning the knuckles over as you do this.

Figure 6-C

Repeat the movement by drawing the right fist in and slowly punching outwards with the left hand.

Preschoolers practising 'Star Fists'.

Preschoolers extending the arms to form a punching movement.

Movement 7: The bird (The butterfly)

★ Begin in the Horse Riding Stance.

★ Inhale, crossing hands at wrists, palms up to chest height (see Figure 7-A).

★ Exhale as you uncross your hands, raising them to the sides, palms down, at shoulder height (see Figure 7-B).

★ Repeat this movement several times.

Figure 7-A

Inhale, cross hands at wrists, moving your palms up to the chest.

Figure 7-B

Raise your arms to the sides, palms down, at shoulder height.

Movement 8: Stepping and bouncing a ball

★ Begin in the Horse Riding Stance (see Figure 8-A).

★ Inhale as you raise the right arm up to just above shoulder height, raising your right knee up at the same time.

★ Exhale as you lower your right arm and your right leg (see Figure 8-B).

★ Repeat to the other side. Inhale as you raise your left arm to just above shoulder height and raise your left knee and left arm at the same time.

★ Exhale as you lower your left hand and left knee (see Figure 8-C).

★ Repeat the movement several times, imagining that you are bouncing a large ball in front of you.

Figure 8-A

Begin in the Horse Riding Stance and then begin to bend your right leg, ready to raise it off the ground.

Figure 8-B

Inhale and raise your right arm and right knee at the same time (pretending you are bouncing a ball). Exhale.

Figure 8-C

Reverse the movement by raising the left arm and left knee slowly as you inhale. Exhale.

Movement 9: Spinning silken threads from the bottom of the ocean

★ Begin in the Horse Riding Stance.

★ Bring weight to your right side. Bend right knee over your right foot.

★ Inhale as you raise your right arm (palm down) out to shoulder height (see Figure 9-A).

★ Exhale as you lower your right arm, come through the centre to Horse Riding Stance and repeat with weight on left leg, left knee bent, raising left arm to shoulder height (see Figure 9-B).

★ Repeat to both sides several times.

Figure 9-A

Bring your weight to your right side. Raise your right arm and bend your right knee over your toes.

Figure 9-B

Reverse the movement by raising your left arm and bending your left knee over your toes.

Katherine demonstrating 'Spinning silken threads'.

Movement 10: Salute to the sun

★ Begin with feet nearly together.

★ Place hands in prayer position at chest height (see Figure 10-A).

★ Raise hands up past face, release and stretch hands above head, palms facing forward as you inhale (see Figure 10-B).

★ Exhale as you bend your body slowly down to touch the floor with your finger tips.

★ Look down (lower head) (see Figure 10-C).

★ Slowly unfurl your body until you reach standing position.

★ Place your hands back in prayer position.

★ Breathe in and out naturally for this part of the movement (see Figure 10-A).

★ Repeat this movement several times.

Figure 10-A

Place hands in prayer position at chest height. Your feet are nearly together.

Figure 10-B

Inhale as you stretch your arms above your head, palms facing forward.

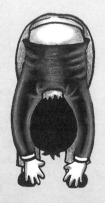

Figure 10-C

Exhale and bend down slowly to touch the floor with your fingertips.

Katherine, Mark and Joshua prepare for Tai Chi outdoors with the 'sun and moon' bow.

A preschooler prepares for her Tai Chi practice with a 'sun and moon' bow.

Relaxation and Visualisation

'I really like lying down doing relaxation. The cushion is really big and I feel good on that big pillow.' (Boy aged 4 years)

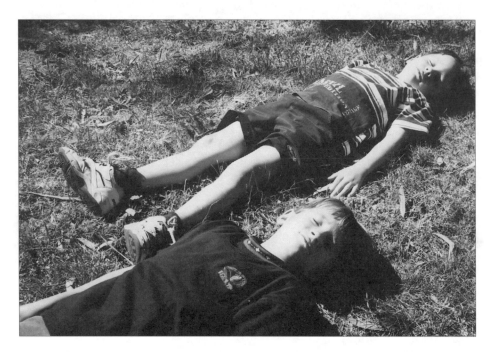

Mark and Joshua doing a visualisation exercise in the outdoors.

What is progressive relaxation?

Relaxation is a way of producing a quiet body and calm mind. Madders (1987, p 27) believes that learning to relax involves becoming aware of the difference between muscle tension and muscle relaxation. She asserts that it is not possible to feel agitated and relaxed at the same time.

Progressive relaxation was developed by Jacobsen (1938, 1970) and is the most widely used relaxation procedure. It involves focusing the attention on body parts and using the breathing to help the muscles relax. Alternatively, the body parts or muscle groups can be progressively tensed and relaxed in turn, using the breath.

When using relaxation with children, it is important to keep the process simple and use terminology that children can relate to (Madders, 1987; Crook, 1988; Mackie, 1981).

What is visualisation?

Visualisation (or guided imagery) is a process used with young children whereby they are asked to lie down, take some relaxing breaths, close their eyes and engage in an exercise led by their teacher or a parent. Through the process we create a story or scene in the children's imaginations (Thomas, 1994).

The visualisation scripts — usually focusing on scenes from nature, imaginary friends, animals or symbols of relaxation — allow the children to participate in their imaginations/thoughts and with their feelings, in a non-threatening way.

At the end of the visualisation process, the children are gently encouraged to bring their awareness back to the room and provision is made for follow-up discussion and expression in a variety of ways (Pearson and Nolan, 1991; Crook, 1988; Murdoch, 1987).

Visualisation techniques follow on naturally from the progressive relaxation techniques (Thomas, 1994). It is important to provide a quiet time for children each day. They learn to value quiet, peace, stillness and reflection. It gives them 'time out' from busy routines and over-stimulation from noise and 'hurried life'.

Joshua, Kate and Mark enjoying a quiet, meditative time in the backyard.

Ideas for spoken directions for a progressive relaxation exercise

The directions are spaced with appropriate pauses. They can be shortened or lengthened depending on the needs of the particular group. They are also suited to working with a single child.

Now is the time to begin playing your relaxation music if you choose to. You might use the following script sequence as a guide to leading your children through progressive relaxation.

★ 'Feel your whole body resting on the floor. Try to allow your hands and feet to be very still. Now, with the help of your breathing, we are going to gradually let your body relax. Try to feel your breathing. Feel the flow of your breath entering your body and leaving it again. As you breathe out, you let go … relax … allow this relaxed feeling to become stronger and stronger, deeper and deeper.'

★ 'Now feel that your very light, soft breathing is allowing you to relax more and more.'

Encourage efforts by comments like 'You are doing very well.', 'I'm pleased to see everyone lying so still and listening well.'. This is very important and reassuring for the children.

★ 'Now try to feel your body parts. Feel your feet and toes. Can you feel your toenails? Breathe in and curl your toes under very tightly — this is tension — now let them unwind as you breathe out and feel your feet relaxing … feel the tension leave every part of your body. Relax your ankles, breathing in and out.'

★ 'Feel the lower part of your legs between your knees and your ankles. Can you feel the weight of your legs as they press against the floor?'

★ 'As you breathe out, just let the lower part of your legs relax. Relax your knees. Breathe in and move your attention to the tops of your legs and see if you can feel those big muscles there. Let them relax … let them become soft and flowing as you breathe out. Feel the whole length of your legs very relaxed.'

★ 'Breathe in and relax your bottom … let your bottom feel as if it is sinking into the carpet … breathe out.'

★ 'Now feel right along your back … try to feel the part of your back which doesn't quite touch the floor … feel yourself stretching out taller as you lie there. Breathe in.'

★ 'Can you feel the very soft movement of your breathing in your back? Can you be so quiet inside yourself that you can feel the movement of each breath as it flows in and out of your back?'

★ 'Now as you breathe out, allow your back to relax completely … sinking into the floor. Just let your back melt … really try to feel that lovely relaxed feeling coming into your back now. Feel your shoulders relax as you breathe in and out.'

★ 'Relax your arms, elbows, wrists, hands and fingers as you slowly breathe in and out.'

★ 'Relax your head, your forehead, your eyes, your nose and your mouth as you slowly and gently breathe in and out.'

★ 'You are all doing very well. Try to keep that relaxed feeling as you lie on your space on the floor … we are all now going on a journey in our imaginations.'

Now turn to one of the visualisation scripts

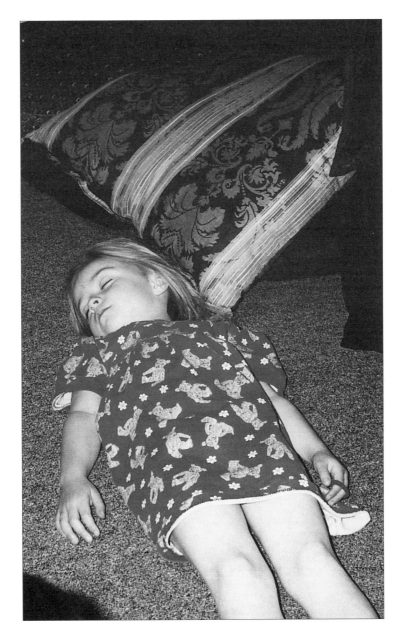

A preschooler relaxes during a visualisation session.

Visualisation script 1: A walk in the rainforest

★ 'As you are lying in this place of peace and relaxation, I want you to come for a walk with me in your imagination. We are going to walk out of this room, through the playground, until you come to a beautiful forest path. As you begin to walk down your forest path, you start to hear the sounds of the forest — the birds calling and singing to each other, the rustling of the breeze through the trees and some water flowing in the distance. As you walk down your forest path notice the beautiful tall trees that lead you down. You know that you are very safe and secure while you are on this journey … we are all here to look after you.'

★ 'You are not wearing any shoes and you can feel the dirt and leaves under your feet — and it feels good. Feel the gentle sun shining down on your face and feel the breeze whisper through your hair.'

★ 'As you walk along, notice the beautiful flowers, ferns and trees growing in the forest. What colours are there in your forest?'

★ 'Look up into the trees and watch the birds flying from branch to branch. What kinds of birds do you have in your forest?'

★ 'Now, the sound of rushing water is becoming louder as you walk further down your forest path. You notice a beautiful forest pool being filled by a magical waterfall. Sit down on a rock beside your pool and feel the water trickling over your feet.'

★ 'Sit beside your forest pool for a short while now.'

★ 'What noises can you hear, sitting beside your pool?'

★ 'Look around at the beautiful plants, rocks, mosses and ferns. Listen to the music and sit quietly by the pool for a while.' (Pause for a short time.)

★ 'Now … we know it's time to leave our forest pool, but because this is a place that we have created in our imaginations, we can return here any time we wish.'

★ 'But … for now … stand up from your rock and take one last look at this forest pool and begin walking back up your forest path.'

★ 'Make your way to the top of the path now and return to our building, through the playground and the gardens, up to the door and into our room.'

★ 'Now … still with your eyes closed, think about how you feel right now … are you relaxed and at peace? Think back to some of the lovely things you saw and felt in your rainforest.'

★ 'Now … gradually bring your mind back to our room and slowly bring your body out of the relaxation. Begin to wiggle your fingers and toes, gently move your body from side to side and slowly open your eyes. When you are ready, slowly sit up and look around the room and at everyone else who has been on this journey with you. How do you feel?'

★ 'What a wonderful journey! You did very well!'

★ 'We are now going to talk a little about our forest walk …'

'The forest is full of animals.' (Girl aged 6 years)

Visualisation 2: My magical rainforest friend

★ 'As you are lying here, beginning to feel more and more relaxed and at peace, I want you to imagine that we are walking out of the room and taking our path down to the beautiful rainforest that we have visited before. Look up at all of the beautiful tall trees as you pass.'

★ 'What smells and sounds are in your forest today? Can you hear the birds singing? What kinds of birds are in your forest? What colours are your birds? Can you smell the beautiful smells of the forest?'

★ 'What trees and plants can you see today? Are there any flowers here?'

★ 'It feels good to be in this place. This is your special place ... a place to enjoy, a place to relax and a place to dream. You are very safe with all of us around you and you are free to wander in your imagination.'

★ 'You now find that you have come to your magical forest pond. Sit down on your rock and look into the calm, clear water. Quietly look into the depths of the water.'

★ 'You notice, on the other side of the pond, that a beautiful creature has come out of the forest to take a drink. What kind of creature is it there ... on the other side of the pond? It is very gentle and peaceful and it has lovely kind eyes. What is your creature? Is it a bird, another type of animal or maybe a big teddy bear or some other magical character you have heard about in a story book?'

★ 'Say hello to the magical creature with your eyes. Greet it and send it your love. This creature/animal has a very special message just for you. Listen carefully to the kind, secret message it has to give you.'

★ 'Spend a couple of minutes listening to the music, enjoying being happy with your new friend and feeling relaxed and happy to be in this special place ...' (Pause for a short time.)

★ 'It is now time to leave this place for today, so say goodbye to your friend, knowing that you can come back here and spend time with it whenever you wish to.'

★ 'Begin walking up your forest path, taking in all the smells and sounds along the way. What do you notice as you walk back up the path? What do you see?'

★ 'When you get back up to the top of your forest path, turn around and take one last look, and head quietly back to our building. Walk through the garden, through the door, into our room and back to where you see yourself lying down.'

★ 'Before you open your eyes, think about your wonderful, new, imaginary friend and the walk you've taken today. How do you feel?'

★ 'Now, gently begin to bring yourself out of the relaxation by wiggling your fingers and toes. Now, slowly open and close your hands and open and close your eyes. Gently sit up when you are ready. Take as much time as you need.'

★ 'We'll now spend some time talking about our magical forest friend ...'

A forest. (Child aged 6 years)

Visualisation script 3: A flight with a magical bird

★ 'As you are lying here in this place of peace and relaxation, I want you to imagine that a beautiful big bird has come to our door and is asking you to come for a ride with it. What kind of bird has come to greet you? What does your bird look like? What colours are its feathers? What do its eyes look like? Is it an eagle, a dove or some other magical bird that you have heard about in a story?'

★ 'You imagine that you are walking out of the room, outside the door to where the bird is waiting and you climb upon its back. You know that you are safe and secure while you go on this journey in your imagination.'

★ 'The bird takes off gently and flies over our building and above all the houses, schools and shops. The bird flies over the park and we can see the trees, the flowers and the playground as we pass.'

★ 'Our bird flies out over the waves … far out to sea until it arrives at a beautiful island in the middle of the ocean. The bird stops at the top of a big hill and lets you climb down, telling you that it will be back to collect you soon.'

★ 'As you wave the bird goodbye, you notice the ocean from way up high where you are standing. Look at the sparkling water, with the sun glimmering on the waves. As you look out to sea, you see some dolphins diving in and out of the water. How precious these beautiful creatures are. You also notice some seagulls flying through the sky. Enjoy just being here in this place of beauty and quiet and settle in to the happiness, exhilaration and relaxation that comes from being near the ocean.'

★ 'As you are waiting for your bird to come back to collect you, think about all the things that make you such a special and unique person … the way you look, the people you love, your special friends, your faithful pets and all the talents you have that make you the special person that you are. There is no one else in the world who is quite like you … there never has been and there never will be … you are very, very precious indeed.'

★ 'Now … your bird has arrived back on your island and you know that it is now time to leave this place for today. Welcome the bird and climb onto its back … Now … enjoy the flight back to where we came from. Notice the waves, the rocks, the people on the beach. Feel the wind in your hair as the bird soars through the sky.'

★ 'The bird has now brought you back to our building and you carefully climb down. Whisper a goodbye to the bird and know that you can ride through the sky with it whenever you wish to do so. Watch the bird fly away and then return, in your mind, back to our room.'

★ 'Spend a short time, still with your eyes closed, thinking about your amazing flight with the bird. How do you feel? What was it like to go riding over the sea on a bird's back?'

★ 'Gently begin to bring yourself out of relaxation now, by wiggling your fingers and your toes. Open and close your hands and your eyes. When you are ready, slowly begin to sit up and look around the room.'

★ 'We will now spend some time talking about our flight with our magical bird …'

Lying down outside for relaxation and visualisation.

Drawing what the children saw during visualisation is an extension of the practice.

Visualisation script 4: A walk by the sea

★ 'As you are lying here in this place of quiet, peace and relaxation, I want you to come for a walk with me in your imagination. Leave our room and walk out the door, away from the building and down the street. Gradually, you notice that the street is turning into a bush track. Imagine that your track leads you over the sand hills and down onto a beautiful beach.'

★ 'Walk along the sand by the water's edge and feel the water lapping at your feet. Feel the warm sun shining down on you and a gentle sea breeze on your face and hair.'

★ 'Can you see any birds overhead? Are they making any sounds? Can you see any dolphins jumping in and out of the waves in the distance?'

★ 'As you are lying here, try to feel the waves in the ocean … feel the gentle movement of the waves as they flow up and down. Imagine your arms and legs and then your whole body floating up and down on the beautiful clear, blue water of the ocean.'

★ 'Enjoy the feeling of the waves … a floating, relaxing sensation … And the sun shining down on you from above. Notice the cool, relaxed feeling of being rocked by the water in a gentle, soft way.'

★ 'Now let your imagination leave the ocean and just be aware of how your body is feeling right now, as you lay here on the floor. What sensations can you feel in your body? Does your body feel relaxed and calm?'

★ 'Take a short time, with your eyes still closed, to remember your walk to the beach. What did you enjoy about being there? What did you see and hear while you were walking along the beach? How did your body feel when it was rocking like the waves?'

★ 'Now, very gently begin to wiggle your fingers and toes as we start to come out of our relaxation. Gently open and close your hands and open and close your eyes. When you are ready, begin to sit up and look around the room, feeling refreshed and awake and ready to listen to what other people have to say about their relaxation.'

★ 'We'll now spend some time together talking about our walk by the sea …'

Visualisation script 5: A walk to a mountain

★ 'As you are lying here in this place of peace and relaxation, I'd like you to imagine that you are walking away from our building and through the streets nearby. The streets gradually become open paddocks that lead to a path. We begin walking along this path, enjoying the scenery all around us … the trees, the green grass, the birds, the sun and the gentle breeze waving in the branches of the trees.'

★ 'Begin to follow your path as it winds higher and higher up a big mountain. The walk up the mountain path is easy for you and you notice many beautiful rocks, flowers and ferns along the way.'

★ 'When you arrive at the top of your mountain, you sit on a rock and take a rest. What do you see on your mountain? Are there lots of plants? … Do you see any animals, insects or birds?'

★ 'Stay seated on your rock on top of this wondrous mountain and take in the view. What does the sky look like today? What can you see?'

★ 'As you are sitting in this peaceful place remember what a special person you are. Really enjoy the feeling of being in this special place that you have created in your mind.'

★ 'Then stand up and begin walking back down your mountain path. Know that you can come back to sit on your rock on top of this mountain at any time, because this is a place that you have created in your imagination.'

★ 'Feel yourself walking back to our room now and take note of how you feel right now. How do you feel after walking on this great mountain. Take a short time to enjoy this feeling of just being you … while you listen to the music in the background.'

★ 'Now very gently begin to wiggle your fingers and your toes as we bring our bodies and our minds out of our relaxation exercise for today. Gently move your body from side to side and have a little stretch. Open and close your hands and your eyes.'

★ 'Now, very gently, be sitting up and looking around the room, feeling refreshed and awake.'

★ 'We'll now spend a short time talking about our walk to the mountain …'

Visualisation script 6: My symbol of peace

★ 'As you are lying here on the floor listening to your breathing and the music you can feel yourself becoming more and more relaxed. Know that you are very safe and secure with us all as we do our relaxation and visualisation exercises together. This is a time for you to let go, enjoy the quiet and the stillness — and just enjoy being you — you don't have to do anything, be anything or say anything for the next little while.'

★ 'I want you to think of a picture that makes you feel relaxed. This can be a place (like our rainforest) or a very special thing (like a feather, a picture, a plant, a pet or a smooth stone. Paint this picture in your mind as clearly as you can. Try to hold on to this picture in your mind while you are still experiencing the feeling of relaxation and peace.'

★ 'This picture will now become a symbol or picture of peace for you — whenever you think of this picture, you will feel the feelings of quiet, peace and stillness around you. What is your special symbol of peace — is it a flower, a rainbow, a tree or is it something quite different and special to you.'

★ 'Now … spend a few more seconds with your peace symbol and then slowly begin to bring yourself out of your relaxation. Wiggle your fingers and your toes. Gently move your body from side to side and begin to stretch. In your own time, open and close your eyes gently and slowly come out of your relaxation. When you sit up you will be feeling refreshed and peaceful.'

★ 'We'll now spend some time talking about and drawing our peace symbols …'

Visualisation script 7: Floating on a cloud

★ 'As you are lying in this place of peace and relaxation, I want you to imagine that we have left our room and that we have boarded an aeroplane. We are flying way up into the sky and as we hover over the clouds, we slowly begin to climb out of the plane. We step onto the huge bank of clouds outside our aeroplane.'

★ 'As far as you can see there are white, cotton wool-like clouds immersed in bright light from the sun. The cloud nearest to you looks so comfortable that you decide to lie down on it.'

★ 'The feeling as you ride along on this cloud is one of being safe, secure and very relaxed. The soft cloud supports and rocks you as you move through the sky. The feeling of floating way above the earth enables you to feel free, relaxed and at peace. Enjoy this feeling of freedom and relaxation as you lie there listening to the music for a short time …'

★ 'How does your body feel right now? Do you feel calm and relaxed? Are you ready to step back inside the aeroplane now?'

★ 'Allow the plane to carry you back to earth and come back into our room where we are all lying in our relaxation position. Know that you can return to your relaxation cloud whenever you wish to because it is a scene that you have created in your imagination. Magical things happen when we dream, visualise and imagine. We are able to do things that are not possible in real life.'

★ 'Now … begin to wiggle your fingers and your toes … and slowly come out of your relaxation. Move your body from side to side and slowly open your eyes. When you are ready, sit up and look around the room. Feel ready to share your thoughts with us and be ready to hear about the cloud journey that other people experienced …'

Visualisation script 8: White light of love

- ★ 'As you are lying in this place of relaxation and quiet, I want you to gently listen to your breathing and the music. Feel your breathing and your body become soft and loose.'

- ★ 'As you lie there, I'd like you to imagine a beautiful white light flowing out of the top of your head and flowing down all around your body. Try to imagine yourself lying there surrounded by a pool of white, shining, sparkling, soft light …'

- ★ 'This is a light of love, peace and protection just for you. Imagine the light is soothing, healing and warming you …'

- ★ 'Feel the radiance and beauty of this white light flowing all around you.'

- ★ 'Just as this light shines out peace and beauty, so do you. Think of yourself as the special person that you are and imagine your love and peace shining out into the world just as your light is doing.'

- ★ 'Now think of someone you love very much and send some of your loving thoughts to them. Imagine that person being surrounded by white light just as you are.'

- ★ 'Spend a short time enjoying the feeling of being relaxed, at peace and immersed in this beautiful white light. Listen to the music and to your breathing.'

- ★ 'Now I want you to slowly come out of your relaxation, knowing that you can get back in touch with your white light whenever you wish because it is an image you have created in your mind.'

- ★ 'Now bring yourself out of your relaxation by gently moving your fingers and your toes. Slowly move your body from side to side. When you are ready, begin to sit up and look around the room, feeling refreshed and at peace.'

Visualisation script 9: My secret garden

★ 'As you are lying here in this place of peace and relaxation, I want you to imagine your favourite garden. Is it in your backyard, or a park or at a friend's house?'

★ 'Come walking with me in the garden. As you leave our room, you begin to smell the flowers growing all around you. What kinds of flowers do you have growing in your garden? What colours are your flowers?'

★ 'As you continue down your garden path, you come to a grass clearing where you find a seat beside a fish pond. Sit down on the seat and take a look into the pond. What do you see in the pond? Are there lilies, water plants and maybe goldfish swimming around? Take in the feelings of peace and quiet as you sit beside this pond.'

★ 'Do any birds come to take a drink while you are there? Imagine that a small bird is sitting on your shoulder and whispering a message in your ear. What is the secret message that the bird is bringing you?'

★ 'Spend a few minutes listening to the music and enjoying the sights, sounds and smells of this garden.'

★ 'Now, with your eyes still closed, stand up from your garden seat and take one last look at your garden pond for today. You know that you can return here whenever you wish because this is a place that you have created in your imagination.'

★ 'Begin to walk back up your garden path now, noticing the many different flowers and trees that grow here. Slowly walk back into our room and prepare to come out of your relaxation.'

★ 'Gently begin to move your feet and hands and stretch your body. When you open your eyes and sit up, you will be feeling refreshed and ready to enjoy the rest of the day.'

★ 'We'll now spend a few minutes talking about what you saw and felt in your secret garden …'

'My cloud has lots of colours.' (Girl aged 3.5 years)

Visualisation script 10: My boat on the lake

★ 'As you are lying here in your relaxation state, I want you to know that you are safe and protected while we go on this journey in our imaginations. Slowly leave our room and walk through the door outside and into the garden. Follow the garden path until you come to a big, green paddock that surrounds a beautiful lake. There are reeds growing around the lake and the water is clear, blue and sparkling.'

★ 'As you walk along beside the water's edge, you are followed by ducks that waddle along hoping for some food.'

★ 'There are many kinds of birds living near this lake and you can hear them singing and calling to each other. What kinds of birds live near your lake? Some of these water birds will be quite different to the ones that live in your magical rainforest. What colours are their feathers? What noises are they making?'

★ 'As you come to the water's edge, you see a boat, a safety vest and a paddle. The boat is waiting for you to get in and make your way out onto the water. It is very easy to drift along in the boat. The water and the gentle breeze are helping you move along the rippling current.'

★ 'Spend some time here, just enjoying the feeling of floating on the water and taking in the beauty and relaxation that nature gives us.'

★ 'Do you see any fish swimming in the lake? Are there any birds flying overhead? Have the ducks paddled out on to the lake with you?'

★ 'Begin to paddle back to the water's edge and leave your boat on the small beach beside the lake. It will be waiting there for you when next you return to this wonderful, peaceful place.'

★ 'Now, walk back through the garden and into our room. How do you feel after your journey to the lake? Try to think of a word that describes how you feel right now.'

★ 'Now gently move your body in the way that you like to bring yourself out of your relaxation state. When your eyes are open and you are sitting up, we'll spend some time talking about our special boat trip on the lake …'

'I like to feel the sun and the breeze all over me.'

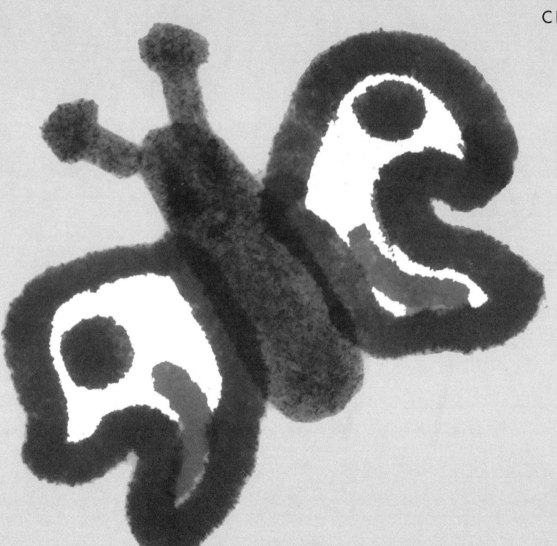

Creative Expression

Forest animal. (Child aged 6 years)

'I really like lying down doing relaxation. The cushion is really big and I feel good on that big pillow.' (Boy aged 4 years)

Building on relaxation exercises through the creative and expressive arts

Relaxation sessions can be concluded by having the children form a 'sharing circle' where each child talks about their Tai Chi and relaxation /visualisation experience. This is a good opportunity to develop listening, sharing and kindness skills. Children learn to be polite and respectful to each other, understanding that each person's contribution is valuable, even if it is different to their own.

The children can describe their favourite Tai Chi movement and tell the group what they 'saw' on their imaginary journey.

It is important for the educator or parent to be open to all ideas and imaginings offered by the children. Similarly, children who do not wish to share their thoughts and feelings on any particular day should be acknowledged and feel free to simply 'be' and listen to the others for a while.

Tai Chi and relaxation sessions can be followed up with a range of creative and expressive experiences such as:

★ drawing;
★ painting;
★ patterning;
★ modelling;
★ story writing;
★ dancing;
★ drama activities; and
★ music.

Ideas for follow-up relaxation sessions are only limited by the imaginations of the teacher or parent and the children.

There is a wealth of ways to bring the lessons of peace, quiet and the reflections gained from relaxation into other areas of the curricula.

The following illustrations show some of the stories and drawings created by children after their relaxation sessions.

'I'm floating on a cloud going to the hundred acre wood where my birthday party is going to be. I feel very happy.' (Boy aged 4 years)

'It's me rowing a boat. I'm just about to get out of the boat and put my feet in the water. This is my boat in relaxation.' (Girl aged 3.5 years)

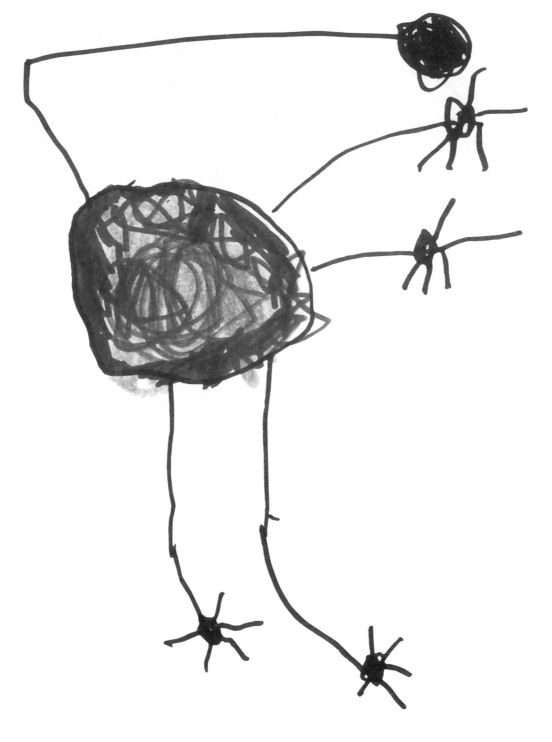

'My head is popping over to see if my hands are doing the right thing in Tai Chi.'
(Boy aged 4 years)

'My garden is on the mountain.' (Boy aged 6 years)

'Me painting the rainbow.' (Boy aged 4 years)

'I like Tai Chi because it's good.' (Boy aged 4 years)

A year 1 boy's drawing of himself doing Tai Chi and feeling relaxed.

General ideas for babies, toddlers and older children

This book follows a specific program of relaxation by starting with warm up movements, Tai Chi and gentle exercises. Progressive relaxation is then followed by visualisation techniques and group discussion of the children's responses. Creative expression activities are then suggested to explore and record the relaxation techniques further. However, there is a range of general ideas that can be used with children that may help 'set the scene' before you embark on the program. These ideas can also be used in addition to the relaxation sessions outlined in the book.

For babies

The following ideas may be used with babies. Experiment with these ideas and watch baby's reactions. Include more ideas of your own:

★ use relaxation music in their rooms (lullabies, nature sounds, quiet chants and soft ambient music);

★ use aesthetics to enhance the environment (soft colours, attractive posters, mobiles, hangings, a relaxation mat with soft toys for soothing activities inside and outdoors);

★ make sure adults use relaxed, calm voices;

★ try aromatherapy such as oil burners, scented lights and mist sprays — make sure you research this for contraindications before you use this technique;

★ use massage at nappy change time, bath time, rest or sleep time;

★ read stories to babies as they sit on your lap;

★ use chewing/soothing toys; and

★ use plenty of cuddles, swaying and rocking.

For toddlers

Use the above ideas suggested for babies as well as the following ones with toddlers. 'Play' with these techniques and modify them according to your toddlers' responses:

★ use music in their rooms (ambient, light classical, relaxation, nature sounds, chanting, lullabies and multicultural);

★ use aesthetics (soft furnishings, quiet corners, posters, plants, mobiles, book areas, cushions, soft toys, draping fabrics, lamps for soft lighting, aromatherapy, float bowls, flowers and plants);

★ use movement to create breaks in your day (for example, before toileting time, recess, moving to another room or activity, before or after lunch — try Tai Chi, bending and stretching, circle dancing, creative dancing, yoga);

★ use relaxing activities (a relaxation mat outside for quiet drawing or playing with soft toys, sand trays, water play, bubbles, private space and time, cubbies, using the garden, relaxation and spiritual books, and transition times);

★ tactile experiences (sand, water, goop, slime, dough); and

★ read stories to toddlers as they sit on your lap.

Life learning

Relaxation time can impart important social learning. The following ideas help children build connection, understanding and respect for each other and their world:

★ listening (poems, stories, rhymes, songs);

★ sharing/waiting/respecting/kindness activities;

★ valuing nature (outdoor relaxation activities); and

★ just 'being'.

Creative expression

Relaxation time can lead children to a wealth of opportunities to explore and develop through the creative and expressive arts. Some examples are:

★ drawing;

★ painting;

★ patterning;

★ modelling;

★ collage;

★ sculpture;

★ drama;

★ dancing;

★ story telling;

★ poems and rhymes; and

★ constructing.

Aromatherapy and simple massage can also be used if appropriate and in accordance with policy and guidelines if in an education setting.

3 to 5 year-olds through to primary school

The above ideas can be extended for use with older children. Build on the list below when developing relaxation ideas for preschool and school aged children:

★ same as for toddlers; and …

★ extended movement and exercise (breathing, warm ups, Tai Chi, yoga);

★ progressive relaxation — learning to relax the body systematically with the breath, valuing sitting or lying still and 'just being', quiet time for music appreciation;

★ visualisation — creating images in our minds to help us relax, making our own relaxation symbol, making up our own relaxation and visualisation 'scripts';

★ listening to extended or serial stories;

★ self massage — learning to stroke hands and face, gentle circles at back of neck, head, lower back;

★ music and rhythm activities reflecting visualisation themes using percussion instruments, soft drumming or rhythm sticks;

★ exploring textures and patterns in a range of materials — scarves, cushions, pieces of fabric that are soft and silky to touch, wool and silk for their comforting, soothing and aesthetic qualities; and

★ developing human awareness and environmental awareness activities and exploring the interrelationship between the two — for example relaxation activities outside such as lying down on the grass for a cloud visualisation; making a 'secret' garden at school based on relaxation and meditation themes; texture touching activities outside; exploring environmental shapes, colours and textures; tree hug; exploring sounds; pet rocks; observation games; environmental I-spy and bingo games — all of these increase knowledge and awareness of self and environment.

A preschooler drawing what she 'saw' during the visualisation sequence 'A walk in the rainforest'.

In conclusion

Relaxation is a life skill that is just as important, if not more, as all the other skills children learn in preschool and school. The ideas contained within this book are designed as a resource and a springboard to further relaxation activities. Adults and children can develop these activities together. It is my belief that the earlier we incorporate 'heart and soul' learning into our curricula, that is, learning how to relax, be calm, content and at peace with oneself, the better life will be for the children in our care.

Learning to relax does not come easily for many adults, so we cannot expect children to learn these skills immediately. It takes time and effort to learn to relax our minds, bodies and spirits through the Tai Chi and relaxation techniques offered in this book.

It is acknowledged that life is fast paced and stressful for many children. The ideas in this book will help children and adults manage their stresses in positive and gentle ways. However, this book is not meant to be a 'fix it' type manual. It is my hope that we can teach children how to relax, be calm, breathe easily, visualise wondrous images and accept themselves and others at an early age. In this way children can be, in some ways, prepared for stress and upset when it inevitably occurs. Many conflicts, worries, illnesses and times of grief unexpectedly appear in all our lives. Many adults struggle to find ways to help them through these uninvited and often unthinkable times. We are often left grasping for reassurance, comfort, peace and inner strength on these occasions. This book will help our children learn to 'act' in positive ways rather than 'react' to their environment and those around them. I see the learning of these skills as creating an armoury that we can use when we are challenged or find ourselves off balance in life.

As well as calling on relaxation skills in troubled times, children can learn positive habits early in their lives and experience the richness and creativity of a fluid, graceful body and an imaginative, active mind. I hope these skills will one day replace some of the mind-numbing and violent activity children witness on television and in video games. If we wish for our children to have hope, optimism and fulfilment in their lives, we surely must help them by paving the way with ideas and practices that enhance these values. The alternative is a life of intellectual and personal mediocrity and impoverishment.

If we care enough about the health, happiness and wellbeing of our children, we will make a commitment to incorporate some of the ideas in this book into the daily lives of our children.

> 'For the cause of
> worldwide peace and harmony
> May it begin in the
> Hearts of children
> And spread'

(Fields and Boesser, 1994, p iv)

Appendix

Some answers to questions and concerns from educators and parents on using *The Magic of Relaxation*

How can this book help me in my work with children?

The relaxation skills outlined in this book integrate the physical, intellectual, social, emotional and spiritual potentials of children so that they can become more responsive to their environment. School and early child-hood centres are currently undergoing rapid change ... not all good in my view. Over-emphasis on competency-based learning and over-reliance on technology are two examples of this change. I believe it is time to bring relaxation skills into wide use in our schools and homes.

How can I fit relaxation time into my busy schedule?

It may be time to re-order your priorities. Are there any routines or less beneficial activities that could be dispensed with? For example, the relaxation program is a perfect substitute for rest or nap time for those children who have grown out of the need to sleep during the day. Do you waste time 'managing' the behaviour of your children? Inclusion of short relaxation times during the day may work as a preventative measure to behaviour problems in some children. The children are settled and focused after a relaxation session. Use this as a prelude to experiences that will require focus and concentration. The visualisation exercises are a wonderful springboard for imaginative story telling and writing, creative expression and communication activities with peers.

Are relaxation techniques 'new age' or religious concepts?

As health and meditative practices from a wide range of traditions are becoming more mainstream in Australian culture, this concern is becoming less prevalent. Inform parents and colleagues about the program by keeping the lines of communication open — hold information evenings, provide written information, photographs and even video footage of the children learning the techniques. Although Tai Chi is derived from Eastern traditions, the movements, as they are presented in this book, do not promote any religious beliefs. I have been invited to present Tai Chi and relaxation sessions in a range of schools and centres with diverse religious backgrounds.

Discuss the lifelong benefits of Tai Chi (or any other gentle exercise), relaxation and visualisation techniques. It always remains an individual's or parent's right not to participate in the program — this should always be respected.

Eastern philosophy, such as Tai Chi, and the relaxation exercises are 'different'

We all need to learn tolerance and acceptance of diversity and difference in our world. *The Magic of Relaxation* introduces ways to embrace this diversity.

Tai Chi exercises are only suitable for adults

This book proves otherwise! Reassure families that Tai Chi exercises are safe and non-invasive. As mentioned throughout, these techniques have been used for many years by myself and my colleagues across diverse age ranges and settings for children. Show them a copy of this book!

The staff do not know how to do the Tai Chi or relaxation exercises

No one needs to be an expert to teach Tai Chi or relaxation to children. After all, we teach music, but many of us are not musicians; we teach drama but many of us are not actors. Learn with the children by following the guidelines in this book. Educators are constantly turning to books and other resources to learn new games, dances, songs, rhymes and poems, science experiments, sporting techniques and drama ideas. It is no different for relaxation techniques. Just give it a go — you'll soon become hooked!

What should I do if the children act 'silly' when I'm trying to get these activities going?

First, you need to be relaxed and at ease — remember, stressed adults cannot help children to learn to relax! Check that you have followed the implementation guidelines set out in this book. Think of how you would deal with 'silliness' during other activities. Would you use an 'I-message' to remind the children of your expectations? For example, 'It is disappointing when people misbehave during relaxation. Let's all listen and enjoy this time together.'

When relaxation activities are introduced to children for the first time, there can be a 'testing of the waters'. The techniques bring with them their own appeal, calm and 'discipline' in a short space of time. The initial silliness will subside. I know this from my rich experiences with emotionally disturbed and behaviourally disordered children over the years.

Of course, some children have 'bad' days. Occasionally a child may just want to sit and watch. They may wish to quietly look at a book on this occasion. Be clear that they are not to disrupt the relaxation enjoyment of their classmates. If a child is particularly angry or upset on any one day, it may be helpful to ask a colleague or parent to undertake another activity with the child away from the group. Teamwork and support for each other helps the relaxation program to succeed.

What should I call these activities?

Ask your children to help you choose a name. In my research, I have discovered a wealth of ideas from 'relaxation time', 'meditation time', 'awareness activities', 'centring activities' and 'quiet time' through to 'Kiddie Quieting Reflex' and 'Head Ed.' (The last two are not my favourites!).

Should we hold a discussion after each session?

It's up to you. Try not to force a 'lesson to be learned' from each session — that is not the point of the program. It is important, however, to allow children time to 'debrief' from their experiences and share their responses (if they choose to) with their peers.

Will I encounter resistance from my management committee, director, principal or school board?

Clearly, you need to seek permission from supervisors and parents before embarking on a relaxation program. Mostly, they will be excited about the possibilities a relaxation program represents. Providing information about the benefits of such a program is always a good start. This book and the references cited at the end will provide ample background reading.

relaxed

Useful references

Below is a list of books and articles I use in my work with children and adults. A few may seem a little 'dated' but the ideas and information they contain are nevertheless valuable.

Armstrong, T. (1995). *The myth of the A.D.D. child*. New York: Plume.

Bennett, V. (1996). *Making dreams come true: visualisations and practical exercises to help children set and achieve their goals*. Sydney: Hodder and Stoughton.

Bennett, V. (2001). *Lifesmart: Choices for young people about friendship, family and future*. Sydney: Finch Publishing.

Chuen, Lam Kam. (1999). *The way of healing: Chi Kung for energy and health*. London: Axiom.

Crook, R. (1988). *Relaxation for children*. Katoomba: Second Back Row Publishing.

Dang, T. (1994). *Beginning T'ai Chi*. Tokyo: Charles. E. Tuttle.

Doe, M. and Walch, M. (1998). *101 principles for spiritual parenting*. New York: Harper Collins.

Eastman, M. (1994). *Taming the dragon in your child*. New York: John Wiley and Sons.

Farhi, D. (1997). *The breathing book*. Sydney: Simon & Schuster.

Farmer, S. (1989). Stress-kids are vulnerable too. *Rattler*, 11, Spring.

Field, E. (1999). *Bullying busting: how to help children deal with teasing and bullying*. Sydney: Finch Publishing.

Fields, M. and Boesser, C. (1994). *Constructive guidance and discipline*. New York: Macmillan.

Galante, L. (1981). *Tai Chi: the supreme ultimate*. New York: Samuel Weiser.

Garth, M. (1991). *Starbright*. Melbourne: Collins Dove.

Garth, M. (1997). *Earthlight*. Sydney: Harper Collins.

Gawler, I. (1987). *Peace of mind*. Adelaide: Hill of Content.

Hay, L. (1984). *You can heal your life*. Santa Monica: Hay House.

Hendricks, G. and Wills, R. (1975). *The centering book*. Englewood Cliffs, New Jersey: Prentice Hall.

Hendricks, G and Wills, R. (1977). *The second centering book*. Englewood Cliffs, New Jersey: Prentice Hall.

Hewitt, D. and Heidemann, S. (1998). *The optimistic classroom: creative ways to give children hope*. St Paul: Readleaf.

Honig, A. (1986). Research in review: Stress and coping in children. In Brown McCracken (1986). *Reducing stress in young children's lives.* Washington: NAYEC.

Hutchinson, F. (1996). *Educating beyond violent futures.* New York: Routledge.

Jacobsen, E. (1938). *Progressive relaxation.* Chicago: University of Chicago Press.

Jacobsen, E. (1970). *You must relax.* New York: McGraw Hill.

Jenkins, P. (1995). *Nurturing spirituality in children.* Hillsboro: Beyond Words Publishing.

Jones, M. (1999). *Your Child — Headaches and migraine: practical and easy to follow advice.* Shaftesbury: Element Books.

Jones, M. (2000). *Hyperactivity: what's the alternative?* Shaftesbury: Element Books.

Khor, G. (1993). *Tai chi qigong for stress control and relaxation.* Sydney: Simon and Schuster.

Lane-Smith, S. (2000). *Calm kids: using alternative therapies to give your child the gift of inner peace.* Melbourne: Thomas C. Lothian.

Lewis, D. (1996). *I close my eyes and I see.* Findhorn: Findhorn Press.

Mackie, S. (1981). *T'ai Chi.* Sydney: David Ell Press.

Madders, J. (1987). *Relax and be happy.* Sydney: Allen and Unwin.

McKissock, D. (1998). *The grief of our children.* Sydney: ABC.

Moore, T. (1996). *The education of the heart.* Sydney: Hodder Headline.

Nagy, L. (1995). *The natural choice guide to aromatherapy.* Sydney: Hodder & Stoughton.

Neville, B. (1989). *Educating psyche.* Melbourne: Collins Dove.

Odle, C. (1990). *Practical visualisation.* London: Aquarian.

Pearson, M. (1998). *Emotional healing and self-esteem.* Melbourne: ACER.

Pearson, M. and Nolan, P. (1991). *Emotional first aid for children.* Springwood: Butterfly Press.

Reid, H. (1988). *The way of harmony.* London: Unwin.

Rice, J. (1995). *The kindness curriculum: introducing young children to loving values.* St Paul: Redleaf.

Richardson, G. (1998). *Love as conscious action.* Sydney: Gavemer Publishing.

Rickard, J. (1994). *Relaxation for children.* Melbourne: ACER.

Roe, D. (1996). *Young children and stress: how can we help?* Canberra: AECA Resource Booklet (3), 4.

Rozman, D. (1994). *Meditating with children*. Boulder Creek: Planetary Publications.

Saavedra, B. (1999). *Creating balance in your child's life*. Chicago: Contemporary Books.

Shepherd, W. and Eaton, J. (1997). Creating environments that intrigue and delight children and adults. *Child Care Information Exchange*, 9, 97, pp. 42–7.

Stewart, M. and Phillips, K. (1992). *Yoga for children: simple exercises to help children grow strong and supple*. London: Vermillion.

Thomas, P. (1994). *Learning for the heart and soul*. Unpublished Masters Thesis; University of Sydney.

Thomas, P. and Shepherd, W. (2000). *Relaxation: Every child's right to simply be. Child Care Information Exchange*, 1,(2000), pp. 42–8.

Walker, P. (1985). *Baby relax*. London: Unwin.

Youngs, B. (1995). *Stress and your child: helping kids cope with the strains and pressures of life*. Sydney: Harper Collins.

Zhou, D. (1984). *The Chinese exercise book*. Katoomba: Second Back Row Publishing.

Useful music selections

There is a wealth of ambient, nature, classical and relaxation music available — these are a few of my favourites.

3 Roses. Dale Nougher. (1994). Larrikin Entertainment.

Australian Lullaby. (1988). Tony O'Connor. Studio Horizon Productions. www.tonyo'connor.com.au.

Dream and Discoveries. (1999). Tony O'Connor. Studio Horizon Productions. www.tonyo'connor.com.au.

Dreamtime. Tony O'Connor. (1999). Studio Horizon Productions. www.tonyo'connor.com.au.

Heart and Soul. (1997). Rhythmist Productions. www.iancameronsmith.com.au.

Inner Tides. Ian Cameron Smith. (1994). Rhythmist Productions. www.iancameronsmith.com.au.

In Touch. Tony O'Connor. (1999). Studio Horizon Productions. www.tonyo'connor.com.au.

Lunar Reflections. Ian Cameron Smith. (1993). Rhythmist Productions. www.iancameronsmith.com.au.

Mariner. (1990). Tony O'Connor. Studio Horizon Productions. www.tonyo'connor.com.au.

Medicine Woman. (1992). Medwyn Goodall. New World Productions.

Music for Mother and Child. Tony O'Connor. (1999). Studio Horizon Productions. www.tonyo'connor.com.au.

Rainforest Magic. Tony O'Connor. (1991). Studio Horizon Productions. www.tonyo'connor.com.au.

Rockpool Reflections. (1994). Andrew Skeoch. Listening Earth Productions.

Tales of the Wind. (1991). Tony O'Connor. Studio Horizon Productions. www.tonyo'connor.com.au.

Uluru. Tony O'Connor. (1991). Studio Horizon Productions. www.tonyo'connor.com.au

White Winds. (1984). Andreas Vollenwieder. CBS.

Index

A

adult
    ecology of relaxation, 8–13
    stress management, 6
aesthetics, 11, 16, 75
affirmations and relaxation, 10
aromatherapy, 12, 75

B

balance, 2–3, 31
balanced development, 23
beginning circle, 20
behaviour management, 22–3
    medication and, 23
breathing and relaxation, 8–9
burn out, 5, 7

C

chi, 3, 31
childhood burn out, 5, 7
children
    affect of information age upon, 2
    learning politeness and respect, 67
    signs of chronic stress in, 24–5
    social learning and, 76
    special needs, 7
    stress factors of, 3, 22–3
    stress management for, 6, 23–4
chronic stress, 24–5
circle
    beginning, 20
    sharing, 21, 67
commitment to relaxation, 9
communication in the workplace, 13
creative arts and relaxation, 7, 67, 76
    examples of illustration, 68–74
crystals, 12

E

early childhood curricula and Tai Chi, 6–7
ecology of relaxation, 8–13, 22
education system gap, 6
educator's role, 18–19, 80
empathy, 9
encouragement, 19

environmental awareness (developing), 77, 79
exercise, 31
    as a relaxation technique, 9
    see also Tai Chi exercises
expressive arts see creative arts and relaxation

G

goals and relaxation, 10

H

harmony, 3
health
    concept of, 3
    reducing risks to, 4–5
herbal tea, 12
human awareness (developing), 77

I

internal exploration, 4, 9

L

language and relaxation, 9

M

medication of children, 23
meditation, 5, 9
muscle tension, 46
music
    for progressive relaxation, 47
    in the relaxation room, 17, 75
    in the workplace, 12

N

naming of activities/movements, 31, 80–1
nutrition and relaxation, 10

P

parent's role, 18–19
    in relaxation at home, 25–6
patience, 2
philosophy of relaxation, 9, 13
plants/flowers in the workplace, 12
positive affirmations and relaxation, 10

posture and relaxation, 9
prayer, 9
progressive relaxation, 21, 46
    script for, 47–8
    spoken directions, 47

Q

quiet time, 2, 5, 47

R

reflection, 9
relaxation
    benefits of, 4–5, 8
    creating space for, 16
    developing an ecology of, 8–13
    in the work environment, 11–13
    incorporated in creative arts, 7, 67, 76
    philosophy of, 9, 13
    restlessness during, 21, 80
    ritual, 17
    room 16–17
    routine, 18
    see also progressive relaxation
relaxation ideas, 75
    for babies, 75
    for toddlers, 75–6
    for 3–5 year-olds, 76–7
relaxation session structure, 20–1
relaxation techniques, 3, 9–11
    for home, 26
    managing stress, 23–4, 78
    response to, 19, 81
restlessness, 21, 80
ritual, 17
room set up, 16
routine, 18

S

school curricula and Tai Chi, 6–7
self-esteem, 2
self-nurturing and relaxation, 11
sharing circle, 21, 67
social learning, 67, 76
space for play, 3
space for relaxation, 10, 16
special needs children and Tai Chi, 7
stress
    chronic (signs of), 24–5
    factors of children, 3, 22–3
    management, 23–4
    transformed into vitality, 9

T

Tai Chi, 3
    integration into curricula, 6–7, 79
    religion and, 79
Tai Chi exercises, 20
    cleansing breath, 28
    stretching the arms, 29
    waist swings, 30
    warm up exercises, 28
Tai Chi movements, 31
    expanding the heart, 33
    holding up heaven, 34
    painting a rainbow, 37
    punching in a horse riding stance, 38
    salute to the sun, 43
    spinning silken threads from the bottom of the ocean, 42
    stepping and bouncing a ball, 41
    the bird, 40
    turning the waist and pushing the palm, 36
    Wu Chi, 32
technology working for you, 13
time management, 10, 79
time out see quiet time

V

visualisation, 5, 21, 46–7
    incorporated in creative arts, 7
visualisation scripts, 21
    a flight with a magical bird, 54–5
    a walk by the sea, 56
    a walk in the rainforest, 49–50
    a walk to a mountain, 57
    floating on a cloud, 59
    my boat on the lake, 63
    my magical rainforest friend, 52
    my secret garden, 61
    my symbol of peace, 58
    white light of love, 60
voice and relaxation, 8, 19

W

water's role in relaxation, 10, 12
wellbeing, 3–4
Western society's affect on relaxation, 2–3, 31
windchimes, 12
work environment and relaxation, 11–13
workplace breaks, 13

Y

yin yang, 3, 31